HEADWAY

WORKBOOK UPPER-INTERMEDIATE

John & Liz Soars

Oxford University Press

Oxford University Press
Walton Street, Oxford OX2 6DP

Oxford New York Toronto Madrid
Delhi Bombay Calcutta Madras Karachi
Kuala Lumpur Singapore Hong Kong Tokyo
Nairobi Dar es Salaam Cape Town
Melbourne Auckland

and associated companies in
Berlin Ibadan

OXFORD and OXFORD ENGLISH are
trade marks of Oxford University Press
ISBN 0 19 433560 7
© Oxford University Press 1987

First published 1987
Fourteenth impression 1993

Filmset in Compugraphic Times and Univers
by VAP Group Ltd, Kidlington, Oxford.
Printed in Hong Kong

Acknowledgements

Acknowledgements are made to the following publishers, from
whose texts the extracts and illustrations listed below have been
taken: Associated Newspapers Group plc for 'Those lazy
husbands' (*Daily Mail*, 10.1.1985); Features International for
'Mystery of the girl who just faded away'; Victor Gollancz Ltd.
for an extract from *Castaway* by Lucy Irvine; London Express
News and Feature Services for 'An 80p. loan . . .' and
'Runaway four go back to father'; Longman Group UK for
extracts from *Lexicon of Contemporary English* by Tom
McArthur; Oxford University Press for an extract from the
Oxford Advanced Learner's Dictionary of Current English;
Private Eye for a cartoon by Edward McLachlan.

Illustrations by: Gray Joliffe, Vanessa Luff, David Murray,
Jim Robins, Paul Thomas

The publishers would like to thank the following for their
permission to reproduce photographs:

J. Allan Cash
Mountain Camera Picture Library
Network
Spectrum
Elizabeth Whiting and Associates

Location photography by:
Rob Judges

CONTENTS

INITIAL TEST

The following exercises test your knowledge of English in areas that you should be familiar with. This does not mean that you must get all the answers right in order to study *Headway Upper Intermediate*. Let your mistakes show you the things that you need to revise.

1 Grammar

Choose the best answer, A, B, C or D.

a. A in   B on   **C** at   D to
b. A in   **B** on   C at   D every
c. **A** to learn   B for to learn
    C for learning   D for learn
d. A There   B They're   C It's   **D** Their
e. **A** for   B by   C in   D with
f. A from   **B** since   C for   D in
g. **A** who   B that   C whom   D which
h. A is   B does   C do   **D** are
i. A other   B another   **C** others   D a lot

j. A in the class of Mrs Stoppard
    B in Mrs Stoppards' class
    C in the Mrs Stoppard's class
    D in Mrs Stoppard's class
k. A is   **B** has   C does   D has been
l. **A** as   B although   C while   D and
m. A a more early train   **B** an earliest train
    C an earlier train   D a most early train
n. A has   B is   C can   **D** does
o. A am   **B** would be   C will be   D was
p. A is   **B** there is   C it is   D takes place
q. **A** said   B told   C spoke   D talked
r. A what are people interested in
    B in what are people interested
    C what people are interested in
    D what are interests
s. **A** ask   B asked
    C were asking   D had asked
t. A starts   B would start
    C will start   D would have started

Back to school on the 7.20

The train arrived (a) ___ Charing Cross Station late, by about ten minutes. Or, as they would say in the last carriage, *dix minutes*. It was the 7.20 from Tunbridge Wells, where, (b) ___ Tuesdays and Thursdays, a group of commuters gets together (c) ___ French. (d) ___ teacher is Mrs Marie Stoppard. She heard about the commuter study groups set up by Learn and Ride, and offered to help. She is French, and works (e) ___ Dupont, the international company, and has been running courses in French (f) ___ 1984.

The first member of the group to get on the train is Colin Dearlove, (g) ___ lives in Tunbridge Wells. He puts a sticker on the window and cards on the table in the last carriage, asking other commuters to leave the seats free for the study group. 'People (h) ___ usually very understanding,' he said. Colin has studied (i) ___ subjects on the train – German, history of art, and geology.

He has been learning French (j) ___ for a year. So (k) ___ Mrs Alice Lester, who works in the City. She has a chance to try out what she has learnt, (l) ___ she has relatives in France.

She normally catches (m) ___, but twice a week goes in later to join the class. Another member of the group, Bill Cunningham, (n) ___ the same. 'I like to use my time creatively,' he said. 'If I didn't do this, I (o) ___ bored.'

Elsewhere on the train another group had been learning bridge, and on Wednesdays (p) ___ a world affairs class. These have been set up by Mrs Angela Ridley of Learn and Ride, with the approval of British Rail. 'Naturally I asked their permission, and they (q) ___ they didn't mind at all.'

She hands out questionnaires asking (r) ___, and who might be prepared to offer their services as a teacher, and forms groups on the basis of the replies. She is hoping to have a class on business management. 'If enough people (s) ___ for it, the class (t) ___ on the 7.33 next month.'

2 Vocabulary

Choose the best answer, A, B, C or D.

a. Could you _____ me some money until tomorrow?
   A borrow   B let   C present   **D lend**

b. She has a very good job. I'm sure she _____ over twenty thousand pounds.
   A gains   **B earns**   C receives   D wins

c. How long does your _____ to work take? _duties trong biến_
   A travel   **B journey**   C trip   D voyage

d. The _____ of living will only go up. It won't go down.
   A price   B value   **C cost**   D expense

e. When you come to stay, _____ some warm clothing. It's very cold here.
   A bring   B carry   C take   D fetch _kiên mẫu_

f. Patience is a kind of card _____.
   A play   B match   C act   **D game**

g. While I was skiing, I _____ and broke my wrist.
   A fell   B felt   C feel   D fallen

h. Are you sure he's _____ the truth?
   A telling   B saying   C talking   D speaking

i. Use your time sensibly. Don't _____ it.
   A spend   B pass   C lose   **D waste**

j. Jump in the car. There's enough _____ for you.
   A room   B place   C seat   D space

3 Question formation

Write a question that asks about the words in italics.

Where does he live?
He lives in *Rome*.

a. _when did they time?_
   They arrived *at 8.00*.

b. _How long did He Stay at the hotel?_
   He stayed at the hotel *for a week*.

c. _what are you thinking about?_
   I'm thinking about *what I'm going to do tonight*.

d. _How many daughters has he got?_
   He's got *three* daughters.

e. _where do they usually have lunch?_
   They usually have lunch *in the canteen*.

f. _How often do you go abroad?_
   I go abroad *once or twice a year*.

g. _How long have you worked here?_
   I've worked here *for ten years*.

h. _what does "to chop" means?_
   'To chop' means 'to cut with an axe'.

i. _what Sort of Soup would you like?_
   I'd like *tomato* soup, please.

j. _who discovered America?_
   Columbus discovered America.

Ví trí

4 Social situations

Write what you would say in the following situations.

a. You are in the street. You need a bank to change some traveller's cheques, but you don't know where there is one. What do you ask a passer-by?

   Excuse me! Could you tell me where there is a bank?

b. You have changed one hundred pounds' worth of traveller's cheques. The bank cashier asks you, 'How would you like the money?' What do you say?

c. You have enrolled at a language school. The school wants you to pay the fees today, but you can't. Explain why not, and say when you will pay.

d. You are in a restaurant. You have asked for a black coffee, but the waiter brings you a white coffee. What do you say?

_____

_____

_____

_____

e. You want to know what is on television tonight. Ask to borrow your friend's newspaper.

_____

_____

_____

_____

f. You're having a party at your house on Saturday. Invite a colleague to the party.

_____

_____

_____

g. A friend invites you to a party, but you can't go. What do you say?

_____

_____

_____

h. You need change to make a phone call, but you only have a five-pound note. What do you ask a friend?

_____

_____

_____

i. An English friend is going to your country on business next week. He/she asks, 'What clothes do I need?' What do you say?

_____

_____

_____

_____

j. You want to buy a good English–English dictionary. Ask your teacher for advice.

_____

_____

_____

Check your answers at the back of the book. In this Initial Test there are fifty marks. Twenty-five is a good score. If you got more than that, well done! If you got less than that, keep trying!

UNIT 1

Verb Forms

1 Matching verb forms

Match a sentence from **A** with a sentence from **B**, according to the tense used. Say which tense it is. (Some sentences are in the negative or question form.)

He works in a bank.
She doesn't smoke. │ *They are both Present Simple active.*

A

1 I don't believe you.
2 Have you been waiting long?
3 He hasn't arrived yet.
4 It wasn't mended properly.
5 How are you feeling today?
6 My office is being decorated at the moment.
7 We got lost.
8 What were you doing last night?
9 This book has been translated into several languages.
10 The post is delivered twice a day.

B

a. It's raining.
b. Did you have a good time?
c. How are these machines made?
d. They were looking for something.
e. He was killed in a car crash.
f. What is ~~being~~ being done about inflation?
g. I've been thinking about moving house.
h. Have you seen Henry?
i. A cure for cancer hasn't been found yet.
j. Where do you work?

1 _1-j present simple._
2 _2-g present perfect continuous_
3 _3-h present perfect simple_
4 _4-e past simple passive_
5 _5-a present continuous_

6 _6-f present continuous passive_
7 _7-b past simple._
8 _8-d past continuous_
9 _9-i present perfect passive._
10 _10-c present simple passive_

2 Active or passive?

Put the verb in brackets in the correct tense, and decide if it is active or passive.

My car ___was stolen___ (steal) last night.

P.S passive

Joseph Ford, the politician who (a) _was kidnapped_ (kidnap) last week as he was driving to his office,

(b) _has been released_ (release) unharmed. He

(c) _was examined_ (examine) by a doctor last night, and

(d) _is said_ (say) to be in good health. Mr Ford

(e) _was found_ (find) walking along a small country lane early yesterday evening. A farmer

(f) _saw_ (see) him, recognized who it was,

and (g) _____ (contact) the police. When

his wife (h) _____ (tell) the news, she said, 'I am delighted and relieved that my husband

(i) _____ (find).' Acting on information received, the police made several arrests, and a man

(j) _____ (question) in connection with the kidnapping.

3 Passive construction

Put the following sentences into the passive, using a personal pronoun as the subject.

Someone told her the news.
She was told the news.

a. Someone will give you your tickets at the airport.

you will be

_____

b. People asked me a lot of questions about my background.

_____

_____

c. Someone usually shows airline passengers how to use a life jacket at the beginning of the flight.

_____

d. If somebody offers you a cheap camera, don't buy it. It's probably stolen.

_____

e. Doctors have given him six months to live.

_____

f. Someone will tell you what you have to do when you arrive.

_____

g. My parents advised me to spend some time abroad before looking for work.

_____

h. Pleased to meet you. People have told me a lot about you.

_____

_____

i. At interviews, people ask you quite searching questions.

_____

_____

j. In a few years' time, my company will send me to our New York office.

_____

_____

4 Simple or continuous?

Use each verb twice, once in the Present Simple and once in the Present Continuous, to complete the sentences.

have
He _____ *has* _____ four cars, all of them Rolls-Royces.

I _____ *'m having* _____ lunch with my mother tomorrow.

a. **think**
What _____ do _____ you _____ think _____ of Stephen Spielberg's latest film?

You're day-dreaming. What _____ are _____

you _____ thinking of _____ about?

b. **expect**
I _____ m expecting _____ an important phone call from America. Could you tell me when it comes?

I _____ expect _____ you're hungry after so much hard work. Shall I get you something?

c. **appear**
He _____ to understand what you say to him, but when you ask him a question, he isn't so sure.

Roy Pond _____ at Her Majesty's Theatre in the role of King Lear.

d. **smell**
Something _____ smells _____ good in the kitchen. What's cooking?

Why _____ are _____ you _____ smelling _____ the meat? Do you think it's gone off?

e. **weigh**
I need to know how much the meat

_____ to know how long to cook it for.

Why _____ you _____ yourself? Do you think you've put on weight?

f. **see**
I _____ what you mean, but I don't agree.

She _____ a solicitor about her aunt's will.

g. **have**

I usually pick up languages quickly, but I _____ difficulties learning Chinese.

He _____ more clothes than a department store.

h. **look**

It _____ as if it's going to rain.
What are you doing on your hands and knees? _____ you _____ for something?

i. **guess**

That isn't the answer! You _____!
Think before you speak!

I _____ you're wondering what I'm doing here.

j. **think**

What _____ you _____ of doing when you leave here?

How much _____ you _____ it would cost to fly to Australia?

5 Gap filling

Fill each gap with *one* suitable word only.

FEED IN ENGLISH, PRINT OUT FRENCH

Once upon a time, (according to a much-told story, a computer was set the task of translating 'traffic jam' into French and back into English. The machine buzzed, clicked, blinked its lights and eventually came up with 'car-flavoured marmalade'. Machine translation has come a long way (a) *since* then. Computer translation systems are now in (b) *operation* in many parts of the world. Not surprisingly, the EEC is very (c) *involved*. With so many official languages, translating and interpreting take up (d) *more* than fifty per cent of the Community's administrative budget. But although the efficiency of machine translation is (e) _____ rapidly, there is no question of (f) _____ translators being made redundant. On the contrary, people and machines work together in harmony. Today's computers (g) _____ of little value in translating literary works, where subtlety is vital, or the spoken word, which tends to be ungrammatical, or important texts, where absolute (h) _____ is essential. But for routine technical reports, working papers and the like, which take up (i) _____ much of the translation workload of international organizations, computers are likely to play an increasing (j) _____. The method of operation will probably be for the machine to (k) _____ a rough version, which the translator will then edit, correcting obvious (l) _____, and where necessary referring (m) _____ to the original.

If machines can translate languages, could they (n) _____ teach languages? Yes, say enthusiasts, although they doubt that the teacher could ever be totally (o) _____ by a machine in the classroom. Good old teachers know best!

6 Derivatives

Notice how a dictionary shows you the words that can be made with suffixes.

> **photo·graph** /'fəʊtəgrɑːf *US:* -græf/ *n* [C] picture recorded by means of the chemical action of light on a specially prepared glass plate or film in a camera, transferred to specially prepared paper. □ *vt* **1** [VP6A] take a ~ of. **2** ~ *well/badly*, come out well/badly when ~ed. **photo·grapher** /fə'tɒgrəfə(r)/ *n* person who takes ~s: *amateur and professional ~ers.* Cf *camera man*, for cinema and T.V. **photo·gra·phy** /fə'tɒgrəfɪ/ *n* [U] art or process of taking ~s. **photo·graphic** /ˌfəʊtə'græfɪk/ *adj* of, related to, used in, taking ~s: *photographic apparatus/goods/periodicals, etc.* **photo·graphi·cally** /-klɪ/ *adv*

The stress often changes in such word families.

'photograph
pho'tographer
pho'tography
photo'graphic

Complete the chart below and mark the stress.

7 Idioms

Here are six idioms which contain a word that denotes a part of the body. Match them with a definition.

1 Keep your fingers crossed for me!
2 I'm pulling your leg!
3 It's on the tip of my tongue.
4 I'll keep an eye on her for you.
5 I can't make head or tail of it.
6 I really put my foot in it, didn't I?

a. I've nearly remembered it.
b. It makes no sense to me at all.
c. I'm joking!
d. I'll watch her while you're out.
e. Wish me luck!
f. I said the wrong thing.

1 _____   3 _____   5 _____

2 _____   4 _____   6 _____

What does a **cheeky** person do?

_____

_____

What does a **nosy** person do?

_____

_____

Noun	Adjective	Person	Verb
'photograph	photo'graphic	pho'tographer	to 'photograph
'industry			
			to in'vent
compe'tition			
'criticism			
		me'chanic	
	'special		
'politics			
'nation			
			to 'analyse
	'active		

8 Verb + preposition (1)

Many verbs are followed by prepositions. Put the correct preposition into each gap.

a. I applied _____ the job that I saw advertised _____ the paper.

b. We hope to have a barbecue, but it depends _____ the weather.

c. I think you're quite right. I absolutely agree _____ you.

d. She got married _____ Peter last week.

e. They are arguing _____ who's going to win the World Cup.

f. The footballer was sent off because he shouted

_____ the referee.

g. You can watch if you promise not to laugh

_____ me.

h. Water consists _____ hydrogen and oxygen.

i. He died _____ a heart attack.

j. Don't worry _____ me. I'll be fine.

UNIT 2

Present Perfect Simple and Continuous

1 Present Perfect and Past Simple

Miriam Field is a writer. Look at the chart of events in her life, and answer the questions. Pay careful attention to the use of tenses — Present Perfect Simple, Present Perfect Continuous, or Past Simple.

Age
6 Wrote short stories about animals
8 Collection of poems published; visit to France and Germany
9 Wrote her first novel (unpublished)
11 Mother died; visit to Italy
18 University
19 First marriage
21 *Mr Bigwig* published (novel)
22 Birth of child
25 *Not The Right Time* published (novel)
26 Divorce; visit to India and the Far East
29 *Hello, Henry* published (novel); visit to America
34 Second marriage
37 Moved to present home in Hastings
38 Began her autobiography
40 (now) Still writing her autobiography

a. Has she had an interesting life? _____

  Why? _____

  _____

b. How long has she been writing? _____

  _____

c. What sort of things has she written? _____

  _____

  _____

d. Which countries has she been to? _____

  _____

  _____

e. State when she wrote these things, and when she went to these countries, using time expressions such as the following.

  At the age of six, _____

  _____

  After the publication of _____

  _____

  After her mother died, _____

  _____

  While she was at university, _____

  _____

  While she was in her mid-twenties, _____

  _____

  _____

  _____

  _____

  _____

  _____

  _____

  _____

f. How long did her first marriage last?

  _____

g. How long has she been married?

11

h. How long has she been living in Hastings?

_____

i. How long has she been writing her autobiography?

_____

2 'How long . . . ?' + Present Perfect Simple or Continuous

Write a question with **How long . . . ?** for the following sentences. You need to decide whether to use the Present Perfect Simple or Continuous. If both are possible, use the Continuous.

a. I live in the country.

How long *have you been living there?*

b. I play a lot of tennis.

How long _____

c. I know Jack well.

How long _____

d. I work in Italy.

How long _____

e. I have an American car.

How long _____

3 Questions in the Past Simple

For each of the five sentences in Exercise 2, write another question in the Past Simple, using the prompts.

a. When _____ move

_____?

b. How old _____ when

_____ started _____?

c. Where _____ meet

_____?

d. Why _____ decide

_____?

e. How much _____ pay

_____?

4 Present and Present Perfect tenses

Put the verb in brackets in the correct tense, Present Perfect Simple or Continuous, Present Simple or Continuous.

I _'ve been learning_ (learn) Italian for three years, but I still _don't understand_ (not understand) very much.

A What are you doing?

B I (a) _writing_ (write) a letter.

A You (b) _____ (sit) at the desk for hours. Is it a difficult letter?

B Yes. I (c) _____ (decide) to resign from my job.

A But how do you know you don't like it? You

(d) _____ only _____ (do) it for a week.

B I do like it. But I (e) _____ (offer – passive) a better one, and I'm going to accept it. It's in Brazil, and I (f) _____

always _____ (want) to go to Brazil.

I (g) _____ (not like) living in cold climates.

A But how (h) _____ you

_____ (know) if you'll like it there?

You (i) _____ (never be) out of England before.

B That doesn't matter. Some friends of mine

(j) _____ (live) there at the moment. They'll look after me.

A You're very lucky, really. I (k) _____ (try) to find a job for months. I

(l) _____ (be) to endless interviews, and I (m) _____ (turn down – passive) each time, but you got two jobs in a week.

B Well, obviously you (n) _____ (apply) for the wrong kinds of job. Don't worry. You'll find one soon.

A I (o) _____ (hope) so.

5 Questions in the Present Perfect

Answer the questions about yourself.

a. How long have you known your teacher?

_____

b. How long have you been learning English?

_____

c. Have you learned any other languages?

_____

d. Have you seen any good films recently?

_____

e. Have you bought a book this week?

_____

f. How much money have you spent today?

_____

g. What's the weather been like recently?

_____

h. Have you been abroad recently?

_____

_____

6 Word order

Many verbs can be followed by a direct object and an indirect object. Usually the indirect object refers to a person, and comes first.

He owes my brother ten pounds.
I bought her a car.

Other verbs like this are:

bring	take	offer	read
show	lend	write	refuse
give	tell	pass	send

The indirect object *can* come after the direct object (with a preposition, usually **to** or **for**) when the direct object is much shorter than the indirect object.

I owe ten pounds to the brother of a friend of mine.

When both objects are pronouns, the direct object comes first.

Give it to me.   *Show it to her.*   *Buy it for me.*

Put the following words into the correct order.

a. him / they / job / the / offered

_____

b. sent / novel / to / the / he / ten well-known publishers

_____

_____

c. teaches / French / Mrs Brown / us / three times a week

_____

d. her grandfather / five thousand pounds / her / left / in his will

_____

e. the baby / the doctor / an injection / is going to give

_____

f. a letter of complaint / I / to write / decided / the editor of *The Times* / to

_____

g. a pen / me / lent / she

_____

h. took / to / it / he / her

_____

i. the letter / showed / anyone that was interested / she / to

_____

_____

With some verbs, there is no choice of order. The indirect object always comes after the direct object.

He said 'Hello' to me.
Not *He said me 'Hello'.*

Other verbs like this are:

explain   describe   report   introduce   suggest

Complete the following sentences.

explain / problem / my wife

I explained the problem to my wife.

j. introduce / new teacher / students

_____

k. describe / criminal / police

_____

l. explain / situation / manager

_____

m. report / theft / police

_____

n. suggest / an idea / friends

_____

7 Guessing the meaning of unknown vocabulary

In these sentences the word in italics is a nonsense word that does not exist in English. Look at the sentence carefully and try to guess its meaning. Match each word with another nonsense word that has the same meaning.

After a *storrup* day at work, it is wonderful to return to the calm of my house in the country.

If I had a *tragoon*, I could easily cut that wood to burn in winter.

It was a cold, *grumfit* November day. Clouds covered the sky, and all she wanted to do was get home to a warm fire.

He *huckled* her hand affectionately, and told her he would love her forever.

I heard a *histit* today that you and Sheila are going to get married. Is it true?

The party was awful. A *pawdry* old man bored me to death for two hours telling me how depressed and miserable he was.

The bank robber looked very menacing, and no-one dared approach him. He had a *zooly* in one hand and a revolver in the other.

Sorry about the mess. The office is a bit *glaimy* at the moment. There's so much to do and no time to do it.

Wait a minute. I can't walk. I've got a *scrummy* in my shoe.

Mag a lemon, add the juice to the mixture, and keep it in the fridge for two hours.

There is a *bagshot* going round that there will be a general election soon, but most people don't believe it.

It's not a very nice beach, actually. There isn't much sand. Most of it is covered in *blotchermers*.

___storrup___ means the same as _____

_____ means the same as _____

_____ means the same as _____

_____ means the same as _____

_____ means the same as _____

_____ means the same as _____

Here are the real English words. Look them up in your dictionary and match them to the above meanings.

dreary = _____

a rumour = _____

to squeeze = _____

hectic = _____

an axe = _____

a pebble = _____

8 Verb 'to be' + adverb/preposition

There are many expressions with the verb to be + adverb or preposition. Complete the following sentences with one of the particles.

away   back   out of   over   up   out   in   off

a. Many people are _____ work in the north-east of England.

b. Don't phone for the next few weeks. I'll be

_____ on business.

c. I should be _____ on the 10th of March.

d. I was _____ all night with the baby. She just wouldn't sleep.

e. It had been a long winter, but at last it was nearly

_____.

f. Soon the spring flowers would be _____.

g. I phoned you, but there was no reply. You must have been _____.

h. Are you sure? I've been _____ all day, and I didn't hear the phone.

i. We're _____ sugar. Could you get some more when you go to the shops?

j. I'm _____ to Italy tomorrow, so I won't see you for a while.

Can you express these sentences in another way?

Example

Many people are *unemployed* in the north-east of England.

9 Vocabulary of literature

The following words (mainly nouns) are related to either prose writing, poetry, or drama. Some words fit more than one category. For each word, put 1 (prose), 2 (poetry), or 3 (drama) in column A, and write a short sentence in column B, using the word.

	A	B
act	3	*A play is divided into acts.*
plot	1,3	*The plot is another word for the story.*
author		
biography		
chapter		
character		
comedy		
fiction		
novel		
novelist		
part		
performance		
poet		
producer		
play		
rehearsal		
rhyme		
scene		
scenery		
stage		
verse		

UNIT 3

Gerunds and Infinitives

1 Gap filling

Complete the following story. The lines show the number of words missing. The words are not always gerunds or infinitives.

He tried _____ *to* _____ _____ *find* _____ a a job.

I'd like _____ *you* _____ to help me.

John Bradley was surprised (a) _____

_____ a letter waiting for him on his desk when he arrived at work. Before

(b) _____ it, he hung up his coat and took out his glasses.

'Dear Mr Bradley,' he read, 'We are sorry

(c) _____ _____ you that your services are no longer required . . .'

He could not believe it. After (d) _____ for the company for thirty years, he had been made redundant, one Monday morning, without

(e) _____ warned in any way at all.

There was no point (f) _____

_____ the letter. The ending was obvious. 'Thank you for your loyalty and dedication over the years, and we hope you will enjoy

(g) _____ more time to spend . . .'

The company wanted (h) _____ to go away quietly and enjoy his premature retirement. He was fifty-two. How could he (i) _____

_____ find another job at his age? He knew that firms were not interested

(j) _____ _____ people over forty-five, let alone over fifty. Could he still

afford (k) _____ _____ his daughters to their expensive school?

He sat back in his chair and looked out of the window, wondering (l) _____ _____

_____ next. He decided

(m) _____ _____ the office as soon as possible. He did not want

(n) _____ to see him while he felt so depressed. So he put on his coat and for the last time closed the office door behind him. He stopped

(o) _____ _____ 'goodbye' to the telephonist, whom he had known for years, and left the building.

Out in the street, it had begun (p) _____

_____. He had forgotten

(q) _____ _____ his umbrella that morning, so he turned up his overcoat collar and walked towards the station

(r) _____ _____ his train home. He didn't know what (s) _____

_____ to his wife. The thought of breaking the news to her (t)_____

_____ feel sick.

2 Adjective + infinitive

Rewrite the sentences, using the adjectives in brackets.

I heard you passed your driving test. (delighted)

I was delighted to hear that you passed your driving test.

a. I learned that your aunt had died. (sorry)

_____

b. He wanted to know where we had been. (anxious)

_____

c. She found that her husband was still alive. (amazed)

_____

d. I see you're still smoking. (disappointed)

_____

e. He learned that he had nearly died. (shocked)

_____

3 Want / tell / ask / make someone do

What does the mother say to her children?
Write sentences using **want you to** . . .

I want you to tidy the room.

_____

_____

_____

_____

Report the mother's words and actions, using **ask**, **tell**, and **make**.

She told them to	
She asked them to	tidy the room.
She made them	

_____

_____

_____

_____

_____

_____

_____

_____

_____

_____

_____

_____

4 Verbs + gerund or infinitive

Rewrite the sentences, using the verbs in brackets.

'Come to the party. You'll really enjoy it,' he said to her. (persuade)

He persuaded her to go to the party.

a. 'Yes, I did drive too fast through the town,' she said. (admit)

_____

b. 'I'll lend you some money, if you like,' he said to me. (offer)

_____

c. 'If I were you, I'd accept the job,' he said to his daughter. (advise)

_____

d. 'Why don't you have a holiday in my country cottage?' he said to us. (invite)

_____

e. 'You must pay for the damage you've done,' she said. So I paid. (make)

_____

_____

f. 'I haven't smoked for three years,' she said. (stop)

_____

_____

g. We needed petrol, so we went to a service station. (stop)

_____

_____

h. I didn't buy food for dinner so we had to go out. (forget)

_____

_____

i. But I fed the cat. (remember)

_____

_____

j. I had piano lessons for years, but I was never very good. (try)

_____

_____

5 'To' used instead of whole infinitive

Notice that the whole infinitive need not be repeated if it is understood.

A You look terrible. You should have a holiday.
B *I'm going to.* (I'm going to have a holiday.)

Write a reply to A, using the verb in brackets.

a. A Why aren't you going to work?

   B (not want) _____

b. A Can you come round for a meal tonight?

   B (love) _____ ,

   but _____

c. A I'm afraid I can't take you to the airport after all. Sorry.

   B (promise) *But* _____

d. A Why can't I take this book from the library?

   B (not allow) _____

e. A Why have you painted the wall black?

   B (tell) _____
   A No, I didn't. I told you to paint it pale yellow.

f. A Did you go out for a meal with him?

   B (not ask) _____

6 Infinitive of purpose

Answer the following questions using an infinitive of purpose.

A Why did you go to the bank?
B *To get out some money.*

a. Why are you studying this book?

   . _____

b. Why do you add salt and pepper to food?

   _____

c. Why do people go on a diet?

   . _____

d. Why would you go to the following places?

   a travel agent _____

   an estate agent _____

   an off-licence _____

   a betting shop _____

   a registry office _____

   a library _____

7 'Talking' versus 'a talk'

Compare the following sentences.

Talking to someone about a problem usually helps to solve it.
I *had a talk* with Susan last night.

The gerund is used when we speak *in general*. To speak about *one specific occasion*, we can use some verbs as nouns in the structure **have a + noun.**

Write two sentences for each of the following words, one with a gerund and one with **have a + noun.**

ride

_____

_____

drink

_____

_____

look

_____

_____

wash

_____

_____

quarrel

_____

_____

walk

_____

_____

8 Vocabulary of professions and people

Complete the chart with the name of the profession and the person (or people) in the profession. (Notice that the root word is not always the same for the profession and for the person in the profession.) Mark the stress.

Profession / area of work	Person / people
'management	'manager
'medicine	'doctor, nurse, 'surgeon
law	
edu'cation	
	a'ccountant
'science	
	engi'neer
	psy'chiatrist
the armed forces	
de'sign	
	'journalist
'public re'lations	

9 Noun + preposition

Many nouns are followed by prepositions. Put the correct preposition into each gap.

a. I got a cheque _____ five hundred pounds in the post today.

b. There has been a rise _____ the number of violent crimes.

c. Have you seen this photo _____ my daughter? Isn't she beautiful?

d. The difference _____ you and me is that I don't mind hard work.

e. I can think of no reason _____ such strange behaviour.

f. It took a long time to find a solution _____ the problem.

g. Could you give me some information _____ train times?

h. I'm having trouble _____ my car. It won't start.

i. She's doing research _____ the causes of tooth decay.

j. This is a machine _____ grinding coffee.

UNIT 4

Question Forms

Survival of the Fittest

'Brilliant!'
(Brian Henderson – The Mirror)

'This is a film
you mustn't miss!'
(Kate Ellis – The Guardian)

Starring Henry Johnson
and Glenda Fields
Music composed by
David Williams
Based on the novel by
Lesley MacDonald
Produced by Dino Valentino
Directed by Michael Camp

At the ABC Cinema,
Finchley Road
Programmes
2.40 6.00 9.00
Late show Saturday 11.15

SECRETARY

Based in Madrid
£12,000 p.a.

Anderson International
is a large firm of accountants,
employing over 1300 people.

We are looking for an
experienced secretary, aged 25–40,
to work in our Madrid office.
He/she must be
bilingual in Spanish/English.

Please send c.v. to:
Personnel Dept.,
Anderson International
Piccadilly, London.

Hampstead.
1920s semi, in
need of some
decoration. Four
bedrooms, two
reception rooms.
Gas c.h. 100 foot
garden. 5 mins
shops and tube,
20 mins from
Central London.
£126,000

1 Questions from advertisements

Look at the advertisements and write questions to fit
the answers.

a. _____
It's an adventure film.

b. _____
Henry Johnson and Glenda Fields.

c. _____
Michael Camp.

d. _____
He said it was brilliant.

e. _____
Kate Ellis.

f. _____
At the ABC, Finchley Road.

g. _____
Three.

h. _____
On Saturday at 11.15.

i. _____
For a secretary.

j. _____
£12,000.

k. _____
It's a firm of accountants.

l. _____
Over 1,300 people.

m. _____
Someone with experience, and aged between 25 and 40.

n. _____
You should send your curriculum vitae to their personnel department.

o. _____
In the 1920s.

p. _____
A semi-detached house.

q. *What* _____
It needs some decoration.

r. _____
100 feet.

s. _____
Not far at all — only five minutes.

t. *How* _____
Twenty minutes. –

2 Questions with prepositions at the end

Make questions from the following statements, asking about the words in italics.

Who are you looking at?
I'm looking at *that man*.

a. _____
She's talking about *politics*.

b. _____
I'm waiting for *the postman to arrive*.

c. _____
He works for *the American government*.

d. _____
I'm writing to *the Prime Minister*.

e. _____
She was angry with *her husband*.

f. _____
The house belongs to *Mr Briggs*.

g. _____
The letter's for *you*.

h. _____
I stayed with *some friends*.

3 Indirect questions (1)

Write some indirect questions about the following newspaper headlines.

Man wins record amount on football pools

I wonder *what he's going to do with it*.
We don't know *how much he won*.

a. **Round-the-world yachtsman returns home**

   I wonder _____

   I'd like to know _____

b. **President resigns!**

   I wonder _____

   I can't imagine _____

c. **Oldest man in the world celebrates birthday**

   We don't know _____

   I wonder _____

d. **Bank robber escapes from prison**

   Nobody knows _____

   I wonder _____

e. **Teachers promised pay rise by government**

   I wonder _____

   I'd like to know _____

4 Indirect questions (2)

Complete the following story, using the reported or indirect questions below.

I had a most strange experience a few weeks ago. I was sitting at home, when at about nine o'clock there was a knock on the door. I wasn't expecting anyone,

so I wondered (a) _____.
I opened the door, and there was this man, wearing an

old raincoat. I asked him (b) __5__,
but he didn't tell me at first. He wanted to know

(c) _____
in the house, which I thought was an odd question.
Anyway, I said I was, because everyone else had gone

out for the evening. Then he asked (d) __2__
_____,
so I said that I wanted to know who he was before I'd
let him into my house, which is only natural, after all.
Anyway, he didn't answer, but looked up and down the
street. By this time I was getting a bit worried, and I

wondered (e) __10 7__,
because this chap seemed a bit suspicious. But then he

told me (f) __5__.
He was a policeman, and he showed me his card to
prove it. He said that the police were watching the
people who lived in a house a few doors away, and he

asked me (g) __1__.
I said I didn't. I'd seen them a few times, but I hadn't
spoken to them. Then he wanted to know

(h) __10__,
so I said 'a few weeks'. I'd seen their furniture van
on the day they moved in. Then he explained

(i) __9__.
He asked me if he could stay in my front room and
watch the street for a while, so I showed him in. I

asked him (j) __3__,
and he said it was because they were suspected of
being drug smugglers. I couldn't believe it. He stayed
for three hours, and then left. Anyway, a few days
later, I read in the paper that the police had arrested
them.

1 if I knew them
2 if he could come in
3 why he was watching them
4 who it could be
5 who he was
6 what he wanted
7 if I should call the police
8 if I was alone
9 what he wanted to do
10 how long they'd been living there

5 Adjective + preposition

Many adjectives are followed by prepositions. Put the
correct preposition into each gap.

a. Are you afraid __of__ snakes?

b. Sweets are bad __for__ your teeth, but fruit is
good __for__ them.

c. She was angry _____ me _____
breaking her best plate.

d. Canterbury is famous _____ its ancient
cathedral.

e. Bill is jealous _____ anyone who has
something he hasn't.

f. I'm very proud _____ my two daughters.
They're so clever.

g. I'm very disappointed _____ you. I thought
I could trust you.

h. You're very different _____ your husband.
I thought you'd be quite similar _____ each
other.

i. Are you excited _____ going to Greece?

j. Many foreigners find driving in Britain quite
difficult. They're not used _____ driving on
the left.

k. Are you good _____ tennis?

l. You are responsible _____ your own
actions.

6 Vocabulary

In the extract from *Audrey Rose* on page 31 of the
Student's Book, there are many words to describe the
way people look, speak, and move.

Example
. . . Hoover (was) **staring** intently at Ivy . . .
. . . he **whispered** sharply.
. . . she **raced** about the small, cluttered room . . .

Ways of looking

Look at the extracts from the *Longman Lexicon of Contemporary English*.

---

face [T1; L9] **1** to look towards (a particular direction) because one's face and body are turned that way: *They faced east. He faced towards the rising sun.* **2** (of a building, etc) to have the front built so as to be towards (a particular direction): *The house faces south/the sea.*

watch 1 [T1; V2, 4; I0] to look at (some activity, amusement, or event) usu while sitting or standing: *Do you often watch television? They watched the games while sitting under the trees.* **2** [T1] to keep one's eyes fixed on (someone or something): *She watched the train till it disappeared from sight.* **3** [T1,3] to look for; to expect and wait (for): *She watched her chance/her moment to cross the street.* **4** [T1.5] to take care of, be careful with, or pay attention to: *I'll watch the baby while you are away. You'd better watch Smith; I think he's a thief. Watch that the milk doesn't boil over.* **5** [T1, 6a,b; V2, 4] to attend carefully to (someone or someone's action): *Watch him jump/doing it. Watch how to do this. Watch what I do, then do the same.* **watcher** [C] a person who watches

notice [Wv6; I0; T1, 5a,b, 6a,b; V2, 4] to pay attention (to) with the eyes, other senses, or mind: *She was wearing a new dress, but he didn't even notice (it). Did you notice me leave/leaving the house? It's good to notice that the price has gone down. Yes, so I've noticed.*

stare [I0 (*at*)] to look, esp for a long time at (something or someone), esp with very wide-open eyes: *She stared at him in surprise. He was staring out to sea. She looked at him with strange staring eyes.*

gaze [I0 (*at*)] to look, esp for a long time over esp a wide distance, esp with great interest, etc: *He gazed at her beauty. The children were gazing at the toys.*

glance 1 [L9] to give a rapid look: *He glanced at his watch. I glanced round the room before I left. She glanced down the list of names. She glanced through the library book. He glanced over the report.* (fig) *In his book he only glances at the difficulties of the new government before passing on to the history of the country.* **2** [I0] (of bright surfaces) to flash as light falls on it/them: *The glasses glanced in the firelight.*

Complete the following sentences with one of the verbs from the *Lexicon*.

a. He couldn't bear to __notice__ as the surgeon began the operation, so he turned his chair

to __face__ the wall.

b. You shouldn't __stared__ at people. It's rude.

c. I was in a hurry this morning. I only had time to

__glance__ at the newspaper headlines before rushing out of the house.

d. She sang beautifully, but she was very nervous —

did you __notice__ ?

e. When he had climbed the mountain, he sat and

__gaze__ at the beautiful countryside all around.

Ways of speaking

Why do people speak in the following ways?

whisper   *People whisper so that others can't hear.*

a. scream

_____

_____

b. cheer

_____

_____

_____

c. swear

_____

_____

d. groan

_____

_____

e. cry

_____

_____

_____

Ways of moving

Tick the boxes to show the differences between the ways of moving. The first column has been completed for you.

	to limp	to stagger	to tiptoe	to march	to race	to crawl
Small steps	✓					
Large steps						
Normal steps						
With difficulty	✓					
Slowly	✓					
Fast						
Quietly						
Loudly						
Without control	✓					

REVISION 1

25

1 In the following newspaper article there are twenty gaps. After some gaps there is a verb in brackets. Put the verb in the correct tense.

Yesterday I _____*went*_____ (go) to the park.

When there is no verb in brackets, put in one suitable word — perhaps a preposition, a verb, a question word, a gerund, etc.

I came to England _____*to*_____ learn English.

Father refuses to stop gaol sentence on stayabed son

Yesterday in York Magistrates' Court, a family drama was acted out in what the judge described as a 'most peculiar case'.

A father told the court that his unemployed son would not get out of bed in the morning (a) _____ look for work, and needed to (b) _____ taught a lesson. Mr Peter Carson (c) _____ to pay the balance of a fine for his son, Jeremy, aged 18, who (d) _____ (send) to prison for 28 days by the Magistrates. Jeremy still owed £56 of a fine of £110 imposed last March for (e) _____ a motorcycle without insurance and without a licence. Mr Carson explained to the court (f) _____ he was not going to help. 'It's pointless. He's such a lazy person that he won't get out of bed to find a job. If he (g) _____ (do), he (h) _____ (be able) to pay the fine himself. Although I've got the money, I won't pay it because I want (i) _____ to realize that you don't get anything in life without some effort.'

Chairman of the Bench, Mr Leslie Samson, said, 'I would prefer (j) _____ to send you to prison as you are so young, but I have no alternative. You're wasting your life in bed when you should be (k) _____ for gainful employment.'

When Jeremy (l) _____ (ask) when he would pay the fine, he replied, 'As soon as possible.' He apologized to the court for not (m) _____ able to pay it, and said, 'I (n) _____ (write) letters of application for six months, but as I (o) _____ (not receive) any replies yet, I feel very depressed. I don't see the point in (p) _____ up early.'

Later his mother, Mrs Barbara Carson, said, 'I wanted him to stay on at school and get some qualifications, but he insisted on (q) _____ when he was sixteen. Some people will say that Jeremy (r) _____ (treat) very badly by his family, but this could be the best thing that's happened to him. (s) _____ to prison will teach him the lesson in life he so badly needs. His father (t) _____ (do) everything he can to help — we can do no more.'

2 In the following letter there are mistakes of grammar and spelling, and some words are missing. Find the mistakes and correct them.

> Hotel Plaza
> West 52nd Street
> New York
> 28 March 1986

Dear Malcolm

At last I am arrived here in New York! I'm very exciting – everything is so big, and people moves so fast. I'm sure I'll enjoy very much.

Actually I stay in a hotel. It's quite, so I sleep all right, not too expensive, and near to centre, wich is very convenient. I think to look for a small flat for to rent. I would prefer live in a flat than a hotel. For me the hotels are not very nice places to stay for more a few days, and in a flat you are more independence.

I didn't tell about my job. I work three days a week as riceptionist at other hotel near to this one, call the Metropole. A lot of people work in the hotel is Spanish or German, and there English isn't very good, too! Yesterday I've bought the book you asked me to get. When do you want that I send it? Tell me it.

Write to me soon. I look forward to hear from you.

Regards,

Ann Marie

3 Put the parts of the sentences below into the correct order.

to the supermarket / every Friday / I go / usually
I usually go to the supermarket every Friday.

a. watching horror films / very much / I like

_____

_____

b. when they are on / usually / I / in bed / but / am

_____

_____

c. to buy / I went / to the bookshop / a friend of mine / a collection of short stories / that / had recommended

_____

_____

d. for his birthday / a silk tie / last year / she / her husband / gave

_____

_____

e. I don't understand / didn't / immediately / you / why / me / tell

_____

_____

f. a newspaper / every morning / most English families / delivered / have / to their house

_____

_____

g. I / remember / never / can / have / put / where / I / the letters / to / that / I have to reply

_____

_____

h. carefully / the report / I'll check / this afternoon / in my office

_____

_____

i. at three o'clock / they're getting married / in the small church / on Saturday afternoon / where / my wife and I / were married

_____

_____

j. five languages / fluently / I thought / she spoke / but / only / she / apparently / three / speaks

_____

_____

8 In the following lists of words, three words rhyme.
Circle the 'odd man out' in each case.

ghost	(lost)	most	post
a. chalk	fork	talk	work
b. due	though	through	who
c. come	crumb	home	some
d. barn	born	dawn	warn
e. done	phone	son	won
f. drowned	owned	pound	round
g. flower	lower	power	tower
h. build	child	wild	mild
i. down	own	sewn	thrown
j. course	horse	force	worse
k. above	glove	love	prove
l. boot	foot	shoot	suit
m. ache	break	shake	weak
n. earth	birth	north	worth
o. eight	freight	height	weight
p. aren't	aunt	can't	want
q. goose	loose	lose	use (noun)
r. rough	sew	though	throw
s. bone	groan	own	shone
t. curry	hurry	sorry	worry
u. blood	flood	mud	wood
v. cows	knows	owes	rose
w. paid	said	maid	weighed
x. doll	goal	roll	stole
y. sung	tongue	wrong	young
z. fear	near	pear	rear

UNIT 5

Narrative Tenses

1 Past Simple and Continuous

Underline the correct verb form.

The flight **lasted** / **was lasting** three hours.

a. It was 8.00 in the morning. A lot of people **stood** / **were standing** at the bus stop, waiting to go to work.

b. A magnificent oak tree **stood** / **was standing** in the middle of the garden.

c. I **studied** / **was studying** politics at university.

d. He **studied** / **was studying** the effects of radiation when he suddenly died.

e. When I woke up this morning it **rained** / **was raining**.

f. It **rained** / **was raining** every single day of the holidays.

g. I asked him what he **thought** / **was thinking** about.

h. I **thought** / **was thinking** the play was extremely good.

i. A What **did you do** / **were you doing** with that electric drill?
   B I was putting up some book shelves in my bedroom.

j. A What **did you do** / **were you doing** with that electric drill?
   B I put it back in its box in the tool cupboard.

k. A What **did you do** / **were you doing** before you took this job?
   B Nothing, actually. I only left school a few months ago.

l. A What **did you do** / **were you doing** in my bedroom just now?
   B The light was on, so I just went in to turn it off.

m. The poor chap **died** / **was dying**. All we could do was comfort him.

n. The poor chap **died** / **was dying** early next moring.

2 Past Perfect Simple

Complete the following sentences, or add a sentence, using a verb in the Past Perfect Simple.

When I arrived home, I was starving. *I hadn't had anything to eat all day.*

a. Tom was furious with Alice because she _____

b. James inherited a small fortune from his father, but a year later he didn't have a penny. _____ _____

c. She was fined £200 because she _____

d. When I saw him, he was pale and shaking like a leaf. _____

e. He was two hours late for the wedding because _____ _____

f. I didn't know her name, but the face was familiar. I was sure _____ _____

g. I couldn't answer any of the exam questions, although _____ _____

h. James was very proud of his eighteen-year-old son, who _____ _____

i. I was very nervous at the thought of catching a plane, because I _____

j. He crawled out of the wrecked car, lucky to escape with his life. _____

_____

3 Past Perfect Simple and Continuous

Underline the correct verb form.

Everybody knew he **had stolen** / **had been stealing** from his employer for years.

a. I knew the facts of the case because I **had read** / **had been reading** the report.

b. My eyes ached because I **had read** / **had been reading** for three hours.

c. The children were filthy. They **had played** / **had been playing** in the garden, and they were covered in mud.

d. I was very nervous at the beginning of the match. I **had never played** / **had never been playing** her before, and I didn't know how good she was.

e. Donald excelled himself as a cook. He **had cooked** / **had been cooking** a wonderful Spanish dish.

f. Donald was very cross. He **had worked** / **had been working** in the kitchen all morning, and no-one had offered to help.

4 Past Simple and Past Perfect

Put the verbs in brackets in the correct tense, Past Perfect Simple or Past Simple.

We missed the beginning of the play, because it

had already started (already start) when we

arrived (arrive).

a. I _____ (not recognize) my old

teacher because we _____ (not see) each other for fifteen years.

b. After they _____ (finish) their work,

they _____ (go) for a drink.

c. When I _____ (arrive) at her house,

I found she _____ (go) out.

d. My brother _____ (eat) all the cake

before we _____ (get) home.

e. I was surprised to hear that she _____ (award – passive) an honours degree when she

_____ (be) only sixteen.

f. When Elizabeth I _____ (die) in

1603, she _____ (reign) for over forty years.

g. After the burglary, nothing _____

(touch – passive) until the police _____ (look) for finger prints.

h. I _____ (write) to the shop to ask

why my books _____ (not arrive) yet.

i. Henry _____ (come) home from

holiday to find that someone _____

(break) into his house.

j. He _____ (refuse) to admit that the

accident _____ (be) his fault.

5 Past Perfect – optional or essential?

In the sentences above, is the use of the Past Perfect optional or essential? For example:

a. Essential: **we didn't see each other** is not possible.

b. Optional: **they finished their work** is possible.

c. _____

d. _____

e. _____

f. _____

g. _____

h. _____

i. _____

j. _____

6 Past, Past Perfect, and Present Perfect

Put the verbs in brackets in the correct tenses.

'Well, you see, Officer, I (a) _____ (drive) down the dual carriageway, when this huge

lorry (b) _____ (overtake) me. I

(c) _____ (travel) at 70 miles an hour, so I've no idea what speed the lorry

(d) _____ (go).

I (e) _____ (never see) a lorry travelling so fast.
Two miles further down the road I

(f) _____ (see) flames and smoke

rising. The idiot (g) _____ (crash) into the roundabout. Obviously he

(h) _____ (swerve) to avoid this boy

on his bicycle.

(i) _____ you _____ (speak) to the boy yet? I think he's all right. When

you (j) _____ (arrive), I

(k) _____ (try) to free the lorry driver. I could smell alcohol on his breath. I think

he (l) _____ (drink). He

(m) _____ (break) one of his legs, but apart from that he's not too bad.'

7 Ordering events in a narrative

Runaway four go back to father

by David Murphy

Finchley railwayman David Barron was reunited today with his four runaway children.

The youngsters, aged between four and 15, left home on Monday in an effort to persuade their mother and father to get together again.

Mr Barron, 34, and his wife Joan, 37, had a row a week before Christmas and she left their home in Walton Street and has not been seen since.

The reunion came after Mr Barron had a telephone call from his daughter Bernadette, aged 13, last night.

Mr Barron spoke to her for five minutes after waiting for the call at a telephone box near the family flat.

Later he discovered that the four children – Bernadette, Christine, 14, Robert, 10, and four-year-old Susan – were staying with a friend of their mother's.

The ex-neighbour had phoned Mr Barron after he made a TV appeal for the children to return home.

Mr. Barron explained how he came home to find a note left on the mantelpiece, written by Bernadette. It read: 'Me, Christine, and Robert have decided to stay with some friends to help you to try and find Mummy. Please try not to worry, as I will phone home. Please try to have Mummy on the telephone to me.'

Early today Mr Barron went to collect the children to bring them home for a re-union breakfast.

'I'm delighted the kids are safe and back home with me,' Mr Barron said. 'We're all a little bit emotional at the moment.'

But Mrs Barron is still absent. 'I just hope my wife will come back and then the family will be complete again,' he added.

In a newspaper article, the events of a story are often not presented in chronological order, but are re-ordered for dramatic effect. Here is a list of events in the order that they appear in the article. Put a number in the box to show their chronological order.

- [ ] Mr Barron was reunited with his children.
- [ ] The children left home.
- [1] Mr Barron and his wife had a row.
- [ ] Mrs Barron left home.
- [ ] Mr Barron had a phone call from Bernadette.
- [ ] Mr Barron discovered where they were staying.
- [ ] A friend of Mrs Barron phoned Mr Barron.
- [ ] Mr Barron made a TV appeal.
- [ ] Mr Barron found a note.
- [ ] Bernadette wrote a note.
- [ ] Mr Barron went to collect his children.
- [ ] They all had breakfast.
- [ ] Mr Barron said he hoped his wife would come back home.

Combine some of the sentences, using conjunctions such as **when**, **after**, **before**, and **as soon as**.

After Mr and Mrs Barron had a row, she left their home.

_____

_____

_____

_____

_____

_____

_____

_____

_____

8 Writing a narrative

Look at the cartoon story.

Write the story about the experiment in two different ways, by taking different events as the starting point of the narrative.
Write *what had happened*, and *what had been happening* before the starting point, then narrate the events. Include information such as the following.

Professor Nesbit and his research assistant, John Trenshaw . . . trying to discover a drug . . . make people more intelligent . . . . . . done many experiments . . . all failed . . . rats died . . . . . . decided to conduct one final experiment one Friday afternoon . . . . . . rat died . . .

Choose two of the following starting points.

a. Research assistant John Trenshaw carried the dead rat out to the dustbin.
b. Professor Nesbit and research assistant, John Trenshaw, were waiting anxiously to see if their new drug would work.
c. The rat in Professor Nesbit's laboratory lay dead at the bottom of its cage.

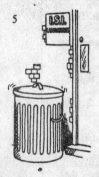

1
'Well, Trenshaw, this is the last chance for our super-intelligence drug XLR6. I've just given the rat the injection.'

2
'Yet another one dead!! That's it. I guess . . . it doesn't work. Take it away!'

3

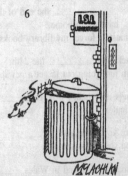

4

5

6

9 Vocabulary of transport

Divide the following nouns into three groups: words related to travel by air, sea, or land. Put A (air), S (sea), or L (land) after each noun. Sometimes the same word will fit two groups.

rails	platform
hangar	roundabout
stewardess	lake
vehicle	oar
cabin	sail
port	bypass
deck	parachute
canal	runway
cart	ferry
pram	departure lounge
cockpit	anchor
boarding card	crew
wings	

10 Prepositions of time

Put the correct preposition of time into each gap.

a. I lived in Paris _____ five years,

_____ 1970 _____ 1975.

b. Beethoven began his musical education

_____ the age of five.

c. We never see our cat. _____ the day it

sleeps, and it goes out _____ night.

d. I don't usually go out _____ the

evening, except _____ Monday evening, when I go to play snooker.

e. Generations of my family have lived in the same

house _____ 1800.

f. A   How long are you staying here?

B   _____ the end of the month. Then I have to go home.

g. I mustn't forget my library books. I must take them

back _____ the 24th.

h. I'm just going out to get a newspaper. If anyone

rings, tell them I'll be back _____ a few minutes.

i. Are you going away _____ Easter, or are you staying at home?

j. I met my husband in Wales. _____ the time, I was working in a travel agent's.

UNIT 6

Expressing Quantity

1 'Some' and 'any'

Complete the following sentences with **some** or **any**.

a. ___Some___ people say that it is difficult to learn a foreign language, but I've never had

___any___ problems.

b. Good morning. I'd like ___Some___ new

potatoes, please. Are there ___any___ peas yet, or is it too early?

c. Why don't you ask the bank to lend you

___Some___ money?

d. Would you like ___Some___ more wine? I don't

want ___any___ more.

e. He never gives me ___any___ encouragement. I wish he would.

f. I made this dress myself without ___any___ help at all.

g. Were you having ___Some___ trouble with your car today? I saw you trying to fix it.

h. Don't worry. If I find ___any___ of your books, I'll send them to you.

i. These aren't my books. Did I take

___Some___ of yours by mistake?

j. Buying shoes is so difficult! I can't find

___any___ that I like.

2 Compounds with 'some', 'any', 'no', and 'every'

Complete the following sentences with a combination of

some	one
any	body
	+
no	thing
every	where

(This exercise includes examples of **any**, **anyone**, **anywhere**, **anything**, and **anybody** to mean *it doesn't matter which / who*, etc.)

a. Put the picture _____. I don't mind where.

b. Does _____ want a game of tennis?

c. What's that noise? Can you hear

_____ screaming?

d. I'm going to the shops. Do you want

_____?

e. You look familiar. Haven't I seen you

_____ before?

f. She left the room without saying

_____.

g. Is there _____ quiet we can go to talk in private?

h. This doesn't look a very nice restaurant. Can't we

go _____ else?

i. I must have asked fifteen people, but

_____ knows the answer.

j. Midas was a king in Greek mythology.

_____ he touched turned to gold.

3 Countable and mass nouns

Rewrite the sentences using the word in brackets. Make any necessary changes.

How much bread have you got? (loaves)
How many loaves have you got?

a. There aren't many jobs for school leavers. (employment)

_____

_____

b. He couldn't give me much information. (details)

_____

_____

c. When I moved into my flat, I had very few chairs or tables or anything. (furniture)

_____

_____

d. There aren't many flats to rent in this town. (accommodation)

_____

_____

e. I haven't got many bags. They're in the boot. (luggage)

_____

_____

f. I had a little time to spare, so I browsed round a bookshop. (minutes)

_____

_____

g. Very little research has been done to find out the cause. (experiments)

_____

_____

h. It's very quiet in my area. There aren't many cars or lorries. (traffic)

_____

_____

4 Few, a few, little, a little

Rewrite the sentences using one of the above forms. Make any necessary changes.

Not many people know the answer to that question.
Few people know the answer to that question.

a. Help yourself to a biscuit. There are one or two left in the tin.

_____

_____

b. My days are so busy that I don't have much time for relaxation.

_____

_____

c. She's exceptionally generous. Hardly anyone gives more money to charity than she does.

_____

_____

d. There's a tiny bit of butter left, but not much.

_____

_____

e. He keeps trying, although he doesn't have much chance of success.

_____

_____

f. 'I'm afraid you need three or four fillings,' said the dentist.

_____

_____

g. He must have made a hundred clocks in his life, but only one or two of them ever worked properly.

_____

_____

h. She wasn't very hungry. She just had one or two spoonfuls of soup.

_____

_____

Those lazy husbands

Men are lazy in the home, according to an official survey published today.

They have about six hours' a week more free time than wives, but play very little part in cooking, cleaning, washing, and ironing, according to the Social Trends Survey by the Central Statistical Office.

Nearly three quarters of married women claimed to do all or most of the housework, and among married men the proportion who admitted that their wives did all or most of the housework was only slightly lower.

The survey showed that washing and ironing was the least popular task among men, with only one per cent performing this duty, compared with 89 per cent of women, and 10 per cent sharing equally.

Only 5 per cent of men prepare the evening meal, 3 per cent carry out household cleaning duties, 5 per cent household shopping, and 17 per cent wash the evening dishes.

But when household gadgets break down, repairs are carried out by 82 per cent of husbands.

The survey says that, despite our economic problems, the majority of Britons are substantially better off than a decade ago. We're healthier, too – eating healthier foods and smoking less.

The average Briton, not surprisingly, is more widely travelled than a decade ago. More people are going abroad for holidays, with Spain the favourite destination.

So here is the way the statisticians see us . . .

Splitting up – the painful facts

There were 162,000 divorces in Britain in 1983, and about a fifth of those involved at least one partner who had been divorced before.

But splitting up is more common among the lower income groups. The survey shows that the rate of divorces per thousand husbands in unskilled manual jobs was more than four times that for professional husbands.

Nearly two-fifths of all currently divorced women aged 18 to 49 were receiving maintenance from their former husbands for their children or themselves.

Marriages in the UK – a total of 387,000 – were three per cent down on the previous year. Just over a third of these were remarriages for one or both partners.

Money

Most people considered that the gap between high wage earners and those on small incomes was too large.

Predictably, people with high incomes were less likely to agree, but even among those with an annual income of at least £15,000, more than half thought the gap was too wide. The majority also disagreed that the rich in this country are over-taxed.

Questioned on Government spending, the three most favoured candidates for extra cash were health, education, and help for industry. The least favoured were overseas aid, public transport, roads, police, and prisons.

Smoking

The number of smokers dropped by around 12 per cent compared with 1972, with more men than women kicking the habit. But drug abuse rocketed. Registered male addicts under 20 doubled between 1982 and 1983.

* There were 56 million people living in the UK in 1983 – only half a million more than in 1971. But the number of people aged 65 or over had gone up by more than two million since 1961, and represented more than 15 per cent of the population, compared with less than 5 per cent at the turn of the century.

Complete the following sentences, using information from the article above.

Women do more work *in the house than men do.*

a. Women _____ free time _____ men.

b. Men _do very little_ housework.

c. _the man hardly_ do any washing or ironing.

d. Only one man in twenty _prepare the evening meal_

e. _17% a few more man_ wash the dishes in the evening.

f. _most_ repairs in the household _are done_ by men.

g. Britons _earn_ more money _than_ ten years ago.

h. Britons _no smoke_ cigarettes, and are eating _healthier foods_

i. Spain _is the most popular_ place to go on holiday.

j. There were _for time_ as many divorces among _professional parent_ as among professional classes.

k. Fewer than two in five divorced women _age 18 to 49 were receiving maintenance from their former husbands_

l. _____ marriages in 1983 _____ 1982.

6 Gap filling

Fill each gap with one suitable word.

Leisure

Watching TV and going for walks (a) _____

the most popular leisure activities in (b) _____.
But although longer holidays and shorter

(c) _____ hours have given people more free

(d) _____, women generally have less free

time (e) _____ men, because they spend

time (f) _____ domestic work, shopping, and
child care.

(g) _____ survey showed that men were

more (h) _____ to read newspapers than

women, while (i) _____ slightly higher

proportion of adults read (j) _____
newspapers than read daily morning national

(k) _____.
More people are taking holidays abroad.

(l) _____ 1971 only 36 per cent of

(m) _____ in Britain had been abroad on

(n) _____, but by 1983 this proportion had

(o) _____ to 62 per cent − nearly fifteen
million people.

7 Writing a statistical report

Write a similar statistical report, either about your
country, or about the members of your class. You
could conduct a survey on one of the following topics.

Sleeping patterns: how long people sleep, when the
majority go to bed and get up.

Most popular evening and weekend entertainments.

Most popular cinemas, theatres, and restaurants.

People's attitudes to an event that is in the news at the
moment.

8 Vocabulary of injury

The following words are often confused.

Verb	Noun	Adjective
to hurt	____	____
to ache	an ache	____
____	a pain	painful
to injure	an injury	injured
to wound	a wound	wounded

People are **wounded** in wars or in a fight, and **injured**
in an accident. Both are more serious than **hurt**.

Ache as a noun is mainly found in the following
compounds: **backache, earache, headache, stomach-
ache, toothache**. For other parts of the body, we say
a pain in my elbow, etc.

An **ache** is dull and continuous; a **pain** can be more
extreme and more sudden.

When **ache** and **hurt** are used as verbs, it is more
common to find them in the Present Simple than the
Present Continuous to describe a pain *now* : *My leg
hurts*.

Fill each gap with one of the words from the chart in
the correct form.

a. The England football captain has

_____ his ankle, and won't be
playing in next week's international against Belgium.

b. The soldier had a bullet _____ in

his thigh.

c. I have a terrible _____ in my chest.

When I cough, it really _____.
d. Two people died and ten were

_____ in a train crash yesterday.
e. I played tennis for the first time this year yesterday.

Today my whole body _____.
f. Two football fans were seriously

_____ in a knife attack by rival fans
earlier today. Three men are helping police with
their enquiries.

g. Please don't touch my ankle. It's too

_____ to move.
h. Doctor: I want to feel your bones. If it

_____, tell me and I'll stop.

9 Vocabulary of food

Divide the following nouns into four groups: kinds of seafood, fruit, vegetables, and meat. Put S (seafood), F (fruit), V (vegetables), or M (meat) after each noun.

crab _____

cauliflower _____

grapefruit _____

chop _____

lobster _____

goose _____

pear _____

cabbage _____

leek _____

grapes _____

pheasant _____

prawn _____

courgette _____

cucumber _____

ham _____

melon _____

plum _____

lettuce _____

mussels _____

pineapple _____

veal _____

raspberries _____

cherry _____

Sunday joint _____

Brussels sprouts _____

What colour are they? Write it down. If they are not eaten raw, how can they be prepared?

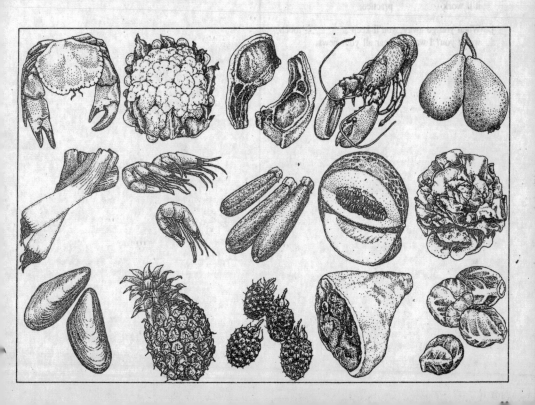

10 Preposition + noun

Put the correct preposition into each gap.

a. I don't think you dropped the vase _____

   accident. I think you did it _____ purpose.

b. At two thousand pounds, the car looks like a

   bargain. It's _____ very good condition.

c. Don't talk to me at the moment. Five bills arrived

   in the post today. I'm _____ a bad mood.

d. _____ average, I spend about thirty pounds a
   week on food.

e. The house was _____ fire, but the blaze was

   soon brought _____ control.

f. As I'm the deputy, I'm _____ charge of the
   office while the manager is away.

g. I can see the arguments for capital punishment, but

   personally I'm not _____ favour of it.

h. Don't give me any money for it. You can have it

   _____ nothing.

i. It's a good idea _____ theory, but I don't think

   it'll work _____ practice.

j. When you go away, you'll keep _____ touch,
   won't you? I want to hear all your news.

UNIT 7

Future Forms

1 'Will' or 'going to'?

Complete the following sentences using **will** or **going to**, and any other necessary words. Sometimes both **will** and **going to** are possible.

a. A I've got to phone a Paris number. Do you know the code?

B No, *I'll look it up*
in the directory for you.

b. A What are you doing over the Easter holidays?

B Absolutely nothing. We *we going to*
rest.
  adv   pron

c. A Did you hear the weather forecast?

B Yes. _____ cold at first, then

_____ a little warmer this

afternoon, and this evening _____
some light showers.

d. A Why did you buy a house in such terrible condition?

B It was cheap. We _____
modernize it from top to bottom, and we

_____
into a restaurant. What do you think?

e. A If you are elected, what _____

your party _____ about
unemployment?

B We have carefully considered this issue. When we are elected, as we most certainly

_____ be, we

_____ create half a million new jobs.

f. A What are you doing here? Annie's expecting you for lunch.

B I completely forgot! I _____ a

ring, and tell her I _____ be
late. Thanks for reminding me.

g. A How will the proposed tax increase on petrol affect your business?

B To be perfectly honest, we haven't thought

about it yet. We _____ cross
that bridge when we get to it.

h. A When is your baby due?

B Next month.

A What _____ call it if it's a boy?

B Thomas.

2 Correcting mistakes of future forms

In the following dialogues, approximately half of the future forms are wrong. Find the mistakes and correct them. Sometimes more than one form is possible.

A What are you doing this weekend? ✓

B Nothing. I stay at home. ✗ *I'm staying.*

a. A I'm terribly sorry! I've spilt coffee on your carpet. It'll stain.

B Don't worry. I'm getting a cloth to wipe it off.

_____

b. A What do you do when you've finished this course?

B I'm going back to Spain.

_____

c. A Have you got a job in Spain?

B No. I'll go back to university. I have to finish my final year.

_____

41

d. A Am I disturbing you if I ring tonight?

_____

B Not at all. I won't be doing anything important.

_____

e. A What time does your train get in?

_____

B At 11.00. If it's late, I'm going to miss my appointment.

_____

f. A Have you decided what you'll do if you don't get the job?

_____

B I do a retraining scheme.

_____

3 Recognizing correct future forms

Underline the future form which is most appropriate.

A Hello, Henry. How are you?
B Fine. And you?
A Not so bad, thanks. Listen I'm ringing to try to arrange a meeting with you. (a) **I'll be coming / I'm coming / I come** to London next Wednesday to see some customers. (b) **I'm going to see / I'll see / I'm seeing** them in the morning. (c) **Will you be / are you / are you going to be** free any time in the afternoon?
B (d) **I won't be / I'm not / I'm not going to be** in London, I'm afraid. (e) **I'll / I'm going / I'll be going** abroad for a few days on business.
A Oh, where (f) **do you go / will you go / are you going?**
B To Germany. I have a meeting in Bonn. My company (g) **will open / opens / is opening** a new office there next year.
A Mmm. Sounds exciting. When (h) **do you go / are you going / will you go?**
B On Monday evening, and (i) **I'm not back / I won't be back / I'm not going to be back** until Thursday morning.
A Oh, well. I could stay overnight and see you then. What time (j) **is your plane getting in / does your plane get in / will your plane get in?**

B 10.40, so if I get a taxi, (k) **I'll be / I am / I could be** in my office at 12.00.
A On second thoughts, don't do that. (l) **I'll see / I'll be seeing / I'm going to see** you at the airport. We can talk there. (m) **We finish / we're finishing / we'll have finished** by 2.00, probably, so then we can have something to eat and I can get the 3.00 shuttle back to Manchester. How does that sound?
B Fine. We'll sort it all out then. Thanks for ringing. Bye.
A Cheerio. (n) **I see you / I'll be seeing you / I'll see you** on Thursday. Have a good trip.

4 Degrees of certainty about the future

Put the verb in brackets in the correct tense. Choose from the following forms.

will might may could won't	do be doing

a. There's no point in phoning him this afternoon. He

_____ (work) in his garden, and he

_____ (not hear) the phone.
b. Don't forget your umbrella. You never know, it

_____ (rain).

c. A I hope we _____ (not disturb) Pat when we drop in tonight.

B Don't worry. She _____ (not work). She told me yesterday she never works in the evening.

d. It's a crazy idea but it _____ (work)
e. A I've invited Jane to the party on Saturday.

B She _____ (not come). She hates parties.
f. A I've bought ten kilos of cheese for the party.
B That's rather a lot, isn't it? They

_____ (not like) cheese.
g. A Why haven't you gone to the airport? I thought you were going to Rome.

B I'm sure the plane _____ (delay – passive). The weather's too bad.
h. Be careful with the dog. She turns a bit nasty

sometimes, and _____ (bite) you.
i. I don't know why I bother with my girlfriend. I

know exactly what _____ (happen)

tonight. I _____ (go) round to her

house to pick her up, she _____

(have) a bath or _____ (do) her hair

as she always is, and I _____ (have

to) wait three hours for her to get ready.

j. I have nothing to wear for this party. All I've got is

this old black dress, and Suzy _____

(wear) something spectacular, as usual.

5 Use of tenses after certain conjunctions

Notice that a future form is *not* used after **if, when, as soon as, until, before, after,** and **unless:**

I'll tell you *when I am ready.* (Not . . . when I will be ready.)
Make sure you tidy up *before I get back.* (Not . . . before I'll get back.)

However, if it is important to show that the first action is completed before the second one begins, the Present Perfect is used:

When you *have read* my book, could you give it back to me?
Of course. As soon as I've *finished* it, I'll give it to you.

Put the verbs in brackets in the correct tense, Present Simple, Present Perfect, or a future form.

a. I _____ (not be) in touch unless

there _____ (be) something urgent
to tell you.

b. The children _____ (not go) to bed

until they _____ (have) a glass of
milk.

c. You _____ (phone) me before you

_____ (go) away, won't you?

d. A When _____ you (go) to the pub?

B When I _____ (finish) this work.

It _____ (take) about another
hour.

e. If you _____ (not hurry) up, we

_____ (be) late.

f. I _____ (come) to London as

soon as you _____ (find) somewhere
for us to live.

g. I'm sure you _____ (feel) a lot

better after you _____ (take) your
medicine.

h. We _____ (have dinner) as soon as

all the guests _____ (arrive).

i. You _____ (not forget) to lock the

door if you _____ (go) out, will
you?

j. I _____ (not let) you go until I

_____ (tell – passive) the truth.
Which of you did it?

6 Verb + preposition (2)

Many verbs are followed by a preposition. Put the correct preposition into each gap.

a. What are you laughing _____? It
sounds very funny.

b. After six months of working overtime, she

succeeded _____ paying off her debts.

c. It took him a long time to recover _____
the injuries he sustained in the car crash.

d. I'd like to complain _____ the manager

_____ the state of my room. It isn't
very tidy.

e. Compared _____ many countries, the
cost of living in Spain is quite low.

f. She was concentrating so hard _____
her book that she didn't hear me come into the
room.

g. Do you believe _____ reincarnation? I
do.

h. Who does that car belong _____? It's in
my way.

i. I dreamt _____ you last night. You were
on a bus going to India.

j. Could I speak _____ you for a moment

_____ our plans for next month? It's
rather important.

7 Reordering a jumbled text

Here is a newspaper article about a couple who won the football pools. The paragraphs have been jumbled up. Put them in the correct order.

An 80p loan wins Gary £400,000 . . . and a bride

a. 'It has always been my dream to go to the church in a horse and carriage, and now I'll have my wish.'

b. They jokingly worked out that each would be entitled to £28.45 a week unemployment benefit.

c. Blue-eyed blonde Sue explained: 'When we first started living together, my parents didn't really approve. They eventually came round, but I didn't see how I could ask Dad for a big church wedding.

d. The couple plan to buy a large house and a new car.

e. Today both will quit their £5,160-a-year jobs as Job Centre clerks.

f. His girlfriend, Sue Palmer, 24, came to the rescue with the 80p he needed.

g. Gary said, 'We always thought we would marry one day, but until now we couldn't afford the sort of wedding Sue wanted.'

h. Gary said: 'Although it would have been a chuckle to walk into the Job Centre and make a claim, we decided against it'.

i. POOLS winner Gary Watson collected his £400,775 prize yesterday – and popped the question to the girl who lent him the stake money.

j. She was paid back in style. As a chauffeur-driven Rolls-Royce was whisking the couple to the cheque presentation at a Birmingham hotel, Gary asked, 'Will you marry me?'

k. They will become officially engaged next Wednesday, the fourth anniversary of their first date.

l. Dole clerk Gary, 24, had only 2p in his pocket when he filled in his coupon.

m. 'We will spend the next year travelling, and may invest in a racehorse.'

1 ___	2 ___	3 ___	4 ___	5 ___	6 ___	7 ___
8 ___	9 ___	10 ___	11 ___	12 ___	13 ___	

8 Nouns and verbs

Write in the nouns for the following verbs. Some have the same form as the verb, and others are formed with the suffixes -ment or -al (with the final e omitted).

Verb	Noun
to aim	
to arrive	
to judge	
to invest	

to approve	
to refuse	
to announce	
to blame	
to delay	
to mistake	
to rest	
to survive	
to develop	
to propose	
to trouble	

In the following group of words, the nouns end in an unvoiced sound (/s/,/f/), and the verbs end in a voiced sound (/z/,/v/). Sometimes the spelling changes.
Look the words up in your dictionary and complete the chart with the words and their phonemic spellings.

Noun	Phonemic spelling	Verb	Phonemic spelling
advice			/ədvaɪz/
	/ju:s/	to use	
		to abuse	
half			/hɑ:v/
			/bɪli:v/
relief			
		to grieve	
	/ʃelf/		
excuse			

44

UNIT 8

Description

1 Relative clauses (1)

Add a relative pronoun to complete the following sentences. If the relative can be omitted, add nothing.

a. If you've got a bad back, the person

_____ you need to see is Dr Clarke. She's wonderful with backs.

b. You can't buy the tablets _____ helped me from a chemist. You have to get them from the doctor.

c. Once I went to an osteopath, _____ manipulated my bones until I felt a bit better.

d. She made me try to touch my toes,

_____ really hurt.

e. My wife and I went to Italy last year,

_____ we spent a very restful three weeks.

f. The hotel _____ we chose overlooked Lake Como.

g. The manager, _____ was a very nice man from Milan, made us feel very welcome.

h. What's the name of the song _____ you're whistling?

i. Wasn't it written by the same person

_____ wrote the musical 'Cats'?

j. He also wrote 'Three Nights in Paris',

_____ the critics disliked, if I remember rightly.

k. The song of his _____ most people

know is 'Teardrops', _____ reached number two in the hit parade a few years ago.

l. Professor Knight, _____ list of achievements includes two Nobel Prizes, will address the meeting tonight.

m. Peter Norrish, _____ nobody thought stood a chance of promotion, was given the job of assistant director.

n. The board didn't even consider my application,

_____ I thought was rather unfair.

o. Anyway, the job _____ I really want is that of director.

2 Relative clauses (2)

Add a relative clause to complete each of the following sentences.

I can't stand people *who keep you waiting.*

a. She's the most beautiful woman _____

_____ .

b. We're looking for a house _____

_____ .

c. The sort of food _____ isn't the same as the sort my mother used to cook.

d. The supermarket _____ has an extensive range of exotic teas.

e. I don't like children _____

_____ .

f. I find people _____ very rude.

3 Defining or non-defining relative clauses?

Non-defining relative clauses need commas round them; defining relative clauses don't.

Punctuate the following sentences according to whether they contain defining or non-defining clauses.
Sometimes the same clause could be both types, but with a different meaning.

a. My wife who works as a journalist is an excellent cook.
b. My daughter who works in New York is getting married soon.
c. The engagement which was announced last week came as a bit of a shock.
d. The man she's getting married to is an artist.
e. It doesn't seem to me that artists are the kind of people who can be relied on to provide an income.
f. Artists who are unproductive are not much use to anyone.
g. My daughter has been married once before which means she should know what she's doing.
h. Her previous marriage which ended in divorce was to a Spaniard.
i. Her mother and father-in-law who were always exceptionally kind were very upset when the marriage broke down.
j. The children who spoke Spanish went to live with their father after the divorce.

4 Spoken versus written style

Turn the following example of spoken English into more formal, written English, incorporating relative clauses where appropriate. The beginning has been done for you.

'I've started a new job, did I tell you? It's as a sales representative with a company. It produces garden furniture, 'Sunnosit', it's called, and it's based in Thornton. Thornton is a small town in the Midlands. The area manager is due to retire next year – he's been with the company for over thirty years. This means, if I do well, I might get his job. One great advantage is having a company car. Well, I have to have a company car, because the job involves visiting different parts of the country. My colleagues are quite ambitious – I get on well with them, but it means the atmosphere at work is rather competitive. I don't mind. Apart from that, the job's fine.'

The job that I have recently started is as a sales

representative with a company that _____

_____

_____

_____

_____

_____

_____

_____

5 Present and past participles used as adjectives

Underline the correct participle.

He told us a **fascinating / fascinated** story.

a. That was a really **disgusting/disgusted** meal.
b. I've always been **interesting/interested** in wild life, especially birds.
c. My husband has the **annoying/annoyed** habit of eating toast in bed.
d. I was **horrifying/horrified** to learn that I had narrowly escaped death.
e. It was a very **embarrassing/embarrassed** situation. I wished the floor could have swallowed me up.
f. He said he was quite **satisfying/satisfied** with my progress.
g. You look **confusing/confused**. Haven't you understood what I'm talking about?
h. Your behaviour was **shocking/shocked**. You should be ashamed of yourself.
i. My exam results were rather **disappointing/ disappointed**. I've got to retake the exams in September.
j. I've just seen a wonderful film about life in space. The special effects were **amazed/amazing**!

6 Participle clauses

Rewrite the following sentences, substituting the relative clause with a participle clause.

There are many endangered animals that are fighting for survival.
There are many endangered animals fighting for survival.

a. The train that is standing at platform 6 is for Doncaster.

_____

_____

b. People who live in high-rise blocks of flats often complain of loneliness.

_____

_____

∴ The money that is given to old-age pensioners is barely enough to live on.

_____

_____

d. The man who had been sent to repair my central heating was totally incompetent.

_____

_____

e. My aunt, who knew how much I liked chocolates, bought me a huge box for my birthday.

_____

_____

7 Present and past participles

Complete the sentences with one of the following verbs in the correct form, as a present participle or past participle.

want	grow	look	stand	hide
steal	injure	cry	say	tear

a. The escaped prisoner was found

_____ in a barn.

b. The room was deserted but for Jan,

_____ by the window,

_____ out as dusk approached.

c. I think I heard the baby _____.
   You go to her. It's your turn.

d. Workmen discovered a vase full of Roman coins

_____ underneath the floor of an old building.

e. I got a letter this morning from the Tax Office,

_____ that I owe them over three thousand pounds. I hope they've made a mistake.

f. Not _____ to wake up the household, I took off my shoes and crept upstairs.

g. _____ up in the country, I learned a lot about animals and their habits.

h. He was caught _____ a ten-pound note from the till.

i. The money _____ in the raid has never been recovered.

j. She fell on the ice, _____ her arm,

and _____ her dress.

8 Intensifying adverbs

Complete the sentences with one of the following intensifying adverbs.

absolutely	rather	terribly
awfully	quite	totally

a. I'm _____ sorry. I won't do it again.

b. The children are _____ starving. What can we give them to eat?

c. I must admit, I'm _____ hungry myself.

d. I'm _____ worried about my exam results. I don't think I've passed.

e. My mother is _____ terrified of flying.

f. Tom's wife had twins. She's

_____ pleased but he's still

_____ shocked. It was

_____ unexpected.

g. I thought the book was _____ marvellous, but I found the film

_____ disappointing.

h. He's a(n) _____ clever man. I don't know how he has such wonderful ideas.

i. Make sure you wrap up warm. Although it's May,

it's _____ cold outside.

j. I think Annie and Jeremy are a(n)

_____ nice couple. They're really good company.

9 Fact and opinion in advertisements

In the following advertisement, underline with a solid line

_____ what is *fact*, and with a broken line _ _ _
what is *opinion*.

This elegant garden trolley is a must for every
household! Designed by our master craftsmen in Italy
and manufactured in Germany, this trolley will grace
your garden, and be the envy of your neighbours! It's
everything you need in a trolley — light and easy to
steer, yet strong and weather-proof, with its frame
made of reinforced, long-lasting plastic and its top deck
finished in non-scratch vinyl.

It has two levels for the food, glasses, crockery,
cutlery, and the rest. The integral bottle recess could
even be filled with ice to keep the drinks chilled. For
the winter months, it can be folded away, but you'll be
tempted to use it indoors! Measures 30″×24½″×30″.

Write a *factual*, objective description of the trolley.

10 Vocabulary and associations

Put the following words in order of size, with the
biggest or strongest at the top.

a. **Water**

pond   _____

• puddle   _____

ocean   _____

lake   _____

sea   _____

pool   _____

b. **Wind**

draught   _____

gale   _____

breeze   _____

hurricane   _____

c. **Accommodation**

cottage   _____

tent   _____

caravan   _____

palace   _____

castle   _____

bungalow   _____

villa   _____

bed-sitter   _____

They are different in size, of course, but what other
differences are there?
What is special about one but not another?

*There are puddles after it's been raining, and they dry
up as soon as the sun comes out.*
Whales live in the sea, frogs live in ponds.

Choose one word from each group. What images and
associations does it bring to your mind?

*Ponds make me think of when I was a child, and going
fishing with my friends and making boats out of sticks,
and falling in and getting wet.*

11 Compound adjectives with numbers

Plural expressions with numbers are found in the singular when they are used as adjectives.

a five-pound note (not 'a five-pounds note')
a six-year old girl (not 'a six-years old girl')

Rewrite the following as compound adjectives.

a. a walk that lasts for three hours

_____

b. a house that would cost fifty thousand pounds

_____

c. a programme that lasts for twenty-five minutes

_____

d. a delay which means a wait of five hours

_____

e. a hotel with five stars

_____

f. a cassette that lasts sixty minutes

_____

g. a bulb of sixty watts

_____

12 Prepositions of place

Put one of the following prepositions of place into each gap.

above	across	against	among
around	behind	below	beneath
beside	onto	over	out of
towards			

a. The cowboy leant _____ the bar in the saloon, drinking a beer.

b. She took her purse _____ her bag and paid the taxi driver.

c. Our cat just loves to curl up

_____ the fire and go to sleep.

d. The view from the top of the mountain was breathtaking. We could see the town and the river

_____ us, and people who looked like ants.

e. Last night the temperature fell to three degrees

_____ zero.

f. The burglar heard a noise coming from upstairs, so

he hid _____ the curtains.

g. The dog jumped _____ my lap, and settled down for a good sleep.

h. The hunter froze as the tiger started running

_____ him. He had nowhere to hide.

i. She has beautiful works of art all

_____ her house, even in the kitchen and the bathroom.

j. These days, politicians like to walk

_____ the crowds, shaking hands and saying one or two words.

k. He climbed _____ the wall and

ran _____ the field.

l. The plane took off and was soon flying

_____ the clouds.

REVISION 2

1 In the following two articles there are gaps.
After some gaps there is a verb in brackets. Put the
verbs in the correct tenses.

Yesterday I _____*went*_____ (go) to the park.

When there is no verb in brackets, put in *one* suitable
word − perhaps a preposition, a verb, a participle, a
relative pronoun, etc.

A surgeon is a person _____*who*_____ performs
operations.

The Island of St Lucia

St Lucia is an island in the Caribbean Sea, forming part of the Wind-
ward Islands group, situated about
twenty miles south of Martinique.
It has a tropical climate.

The French, (a) _____
already ruled several islands in the
area, (b) _____ (settle) in 1650,
and thus beat the English, who
(c) _____ (try) to colonize the
island since 1605. St Lucia changed hands (d) _____ times during wars between Great Britain and
France, (e) _____ ended in
1814 when it was finally ceded to
Britain. It remained in British hands
(f) _____ 1967, when it
became fully self-governing. There
(g) _____ (be) previous
attempts to hand over power in
1924 and 1936, but it was only in
1967 that it lost its colonial status.

The economy is agricultural. The
crops (h) _____ are grown are
mainly for export − bananas,
coconuts and cocoa. It produces
consumer items such as rum, fruit
drinks and soap, but apart from
these there are (i) _____ other
industries. Over the past years
tourism (j) _____ (develop).

Cariblue Hotel
Smugglers Village
St. Lucian
Castries
La Toc
Anse Chastenet
ST LUCIA
Soufriere

St Lucia, the Caribbean island in the sun, is everyone's idea of the
original castaway tropical island, and is definitely the location for those
(k) _____ wish to commune with nature. Dramatically
beautiful, sun-soaked beaches, (l) _____ of the best in
the world, stand at the foot of gently sloping hills
(m) _____ in tropical vegetation. If it is solitude you are
looking for, you (n) _____ (find) it here in idyllic
surroundings; if fishing is your sport, you (o) _____ even
catch a shark, so watch out!

Serviced by direct flights, St Lucia boasts several large hotels,
beautifully positioned, and (p) _____ a full range of
recreational and entertainment facilities. More hotels are being built,
and these (q) _____ (complete) by the start of the season.

There is so much to see and do here, that there is
(r) _____ chance you'll be bored. Your stay on this truly
beautiful island is guaranteed to be memorable.

2 In the following sentences there are mistakes of grammar and tense. Find them and correct them.

a. I asked to the receptionist for help, but he couldn't give me many informations.

b. I had a very nice day yesterday. I hadn't to go to work because it was my day off, so I was going to see some friends instead.

c. Jeremy Peterson, the Hollywood actor, died at home yesterday. He was ill since 1985, and had been having several operations.

d. **A** What do you do tonight?
   B Nothing. Why?
   A Would you like to go out for a meal?
   B What a lovely idea! Where will we go?
   A It's a surprise. I pick you up at 7.00. Is that all right?
   B Fine! How exciting!
   A If you won't be ready, I'll go without you.
   B Don't worry, I'll be ready.

e. The film was very wonderful. I was so exciting. I hadn't an idea how it was going to end.

f. Put your money somewhere safe. You can lose it if you aren't careful.

g. I've had so few free time recently – I think I've forgotten how to relax.

h. I'm sure that's the man who car I bumped into last week. He didn't stop giving me his address, that I found very strange. After all, the accident was my fault.

i. The weather forecast said it's raining tomorrow. If it will, we don't can go out. Never mind. The forecast is perhaps wrong. It often is.

3 Choose the most appropriate linking device from the list below to fill each gap. Write your answer (A, B, or C) in the gap.

The nightmare of population growth

One of the most urgent problems facing us now is the need to control population growth (a) _____ people in the twenty-first century stand a chance of survival.

(b) _____ the birth rate in developed countries has fallen, it continues to rise in poorer countries (c) _____ better medical care. It is hard to understand the phenomenal growth in population that has taken place this century.

Around the first century A.D there were (d) _____ between 250 and 350 million people in the world. Sixteen centuries later, the number had risen to only 500 million. (e) _____, for more than three quarters of the time between Christ and the present day, world population (f) _____ rose.

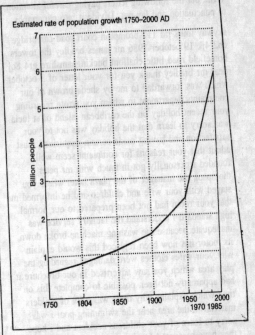

Estimated rate of population growth 1750–2000 AD

(Billion people: 7, 6, 5, 4, 3, 2, 1; years: 1750, 1804, 1850, 1900, 1950, 2000, 1970 1985)

Then, slowly, the rise began. By 1900 it was 1500 million. Now it is 4,700 million. The increase in the past 65 years – less than the average life-time of an English person today – has equalled the entire increase in the previous 100,000 years of human existence.

(g) _____, the rate of increase, now close to twenty per cent a decade, is still shooting up. According to United Nations estimates, the population of the world will have risen to over 6,000 million by the end of the century. (h) _____ the rate of increase is only seven per cent a decade in western Europe, in many developing countries it is between twenty-five and thirty per cent.

(i) _____, population control will be one of the biggest problems facing the twenty-first century. (j) _____ all the warning signs, too little is being done too late.

a.	A in order	B so that	C for
b.	A Although	B Despite	C Because
c.	A because	B despite	C as a result of
d.	A obviously	B probably	C surprisingly
e.	A Therefore	B That is why	C Nevertheless
f.	A greatly	B steadily	C hardly
g.	A Obviously	B What is more	C As well
h.	A While	B Because	C So that
i.	A Personally	B Generally speaking	C Obviously
j.	A Although	B In spite	C Despite

4 Write out the following letter, paying careful attention to punctuation and lay-out. Divide it into paragraphs.

skyway tours ltd 117 brompton court road cambridge cb2 4jk 19 october 1986 mr james bradley the towers homefield road little chalfont buckinghamshire gr4 8qj dear mr bradley thank you for your letter of 3 october which was forwarded to me by sheila brown of our complaints department to whom you wrote regarding your recent holiday on the caribbean island of st lucia i was sorry to learn that the holiday was not to your satisfaction and having made certain enquiries i must admit that your reasons for complaint seem well founded i personally got in touch with mr peter thompson the manager of the plaza hotel where you stayed with your wife and children and he informed me that your room had not been prepared to our normal high standard i understand the laundry service was inadequate because the washing machine broke down its motor has now been replaced this would explain why your wifes clothes were damaged regarding the play area which you saw advertised in our brochure it had apparently not been possible to complete this on time which explains why there was a lot of builders material in the area near the swimming pool i was sorry to learn of your childrens accident and i hope they have recovered from their injuries in view of all these misfortunes i hope you will accept my sincere apologies and a refund of half the total cost of your holiday yours sincerely malcolm green director

_____

_____

_____

_____

_____

_____

_____

_____

_____

_____

_____

5 All the following words have appeared in previous units of *Headway Upper-Intermediate*. Write in the words.

This is what researchers do in laboratories.

___experiment___

a. People and machines are this if you can depend on

them. _____

b. A shirt is this if it doesn't have a pattern; also a person's face is this if it is rather ordinary and

nothing special. _____

c. A sunny day can be this; it's also the money you have to pay if you park your car in the wrong place.

_____

d. This is a bird; it's also what you do to food after

you've chewed it. _____

e. This is what you need if you cut yourself; it's also what a doctor will put on your arm or leg if you

break it. _____

f. If it's a bad cut, you might have to have these; and if your clothes are torn, you put these in with a

needle and thread. _____

g. This is what you do to a cat sitting on your lap; it's

also a sudden illness in the brain. _____

h. This is what your body does if you're cold, or if

you're very afraid. We say 'A _____ ran down my spine.'

i. If you lie in the sun for too long you might get

_____. It hurts!

j. A person is this if he or she is clever and experienced. It's usually old people who are this.

_____

k. If someone helps you a lot, you should feel

extremely _____.

l. If your torch doesn't work, you might need new

_____.

m. Shops have a _____ once or twice a year when they sell things cheap.

n. She didn't just eat half the cake – she ate the

_____ cake!

o. The world's natural _____ are things like coal, oil, and copper.

p. A person is working under a lot of

_____ if he or she has a lot of things to do, and not much time to do them.

q. In the morning the sun _____, and

in the evening it _____.

r. In a bus or train, it's very rude to

_____ at people for too long. They might feel embarrassed and look away.

s. Your _____ are the people who lived before you, usually a long time ago.

t. A _____ is a bad dream.

u. The place where grapes grow is called a

_____.

v. Another word for free time is _____ time.

w. A person who is often angry with others is

_____.

x. Parents hope their children will be

_____ when guests visit or they all go out together.

y. Heroin is a very dangerous drug because it is easy

to get _____ to.

z. Rice, wheat, and maize are all examples of

_____.

6 Below are five stress patterns. Study each one and then match each of the words below to the correct stress pattern. Write the number of the stress pattern after the word.

1 ● ● ●   as in 'century.
2 ● ● ● ●   as in e'conomize.
3 ● ●   as in a'bout.
4 ● ● ●   as in re'dundant.
5 ● ●   as in 'different (only two syllables).

continent	————	interesting	————
Indian	————	vehicle	————
bilingual	————	stability	————
Chinese	————	wondered	————
experience	————	departure	————
competitive	————	several	————
creative	————	chemical	————
developed	————	convenient	————
accurate	————	disease	————
vegetable	————	ancestors	————
biography	————	recipe	————
January	————	statistics	————
colleague	————	medicine	————
successful	————	literature	————
managed	————	depressed	————
emergency	————		

Careful! Some words have fewer syllables than you might think: in standard English *Wednesday* has only two syllables; *comfortable* has only three syllables.

UNIT 9

Modal Verbs of Deduction

1 Deductions about the present and the past

Rewrite the following sentences, using **must**, **can't**, or **might**.

I'm sure Harry's at least sixty.
Harry must be at least sixty.

Perhaps he's having a party.
He might be having a party.

a. I'm sure he hasn't retired yet. He still leaves the house every morning.

b. I'm sure he isn't very well off. His house is in a terrible mess.

c. Perhaps he spent all his money when he was younger.

d. I'm sure he does a lot of gardening. His garden looks beautiful.

e. I'm sure he's read a lot of books about gardening. He's certainly an expert.

f. I'm sure he's working in his garden now. I can hear someone digging.

g. Now I can hear voices. Perhaps he's talking to Miss Appleby.

h. No, I'm sure it isn't Miss Appleby. It's two men's voices.

i. They're shouting. Perhaps they are having an argument.

j. They're talking about money. Perhaps Harry owes the other man some money.

k. Now I can't hear anything. I'm sure they've gone inside.

l. My God! A gun shot! I'm sure Harry has killed him!

m. No, there's Harry outside, so it wasn't Harry who was shot.

n. There's a siren. I'm sure this is the police arriving.

o. Look at all those lights and cameras. Ah! Now I understand. They were making a film!

2 Must or can't?

Reply to the sentences in column 1 using **must** or **can't**, and adding a reason from column 2.

A Is Jane married?
B *She can't be married. She's only fifteen.*

1	2
Is Jane married?	I saw her looking at wedding rings yesterday.
I saw Alice in town yesterday.	I've just seen her playing tennis.
I was served in a restaurant by Tessa.	She's only fifteen.
Is Sheila thinking of moving?	There's a strong smell of paint coming from next door.
Did Anita get engaged to Alan?	She went abroad last week.
Has Pat hurt her leg?	She told me she didn't like him.
Is Jenny going out with Tom?	She's a school-teacher.
Is Mary having her flat decorated?	There's a *For Sale* notice up outside her house.

_____

_____

_____

_____

_____

_____

_____

_____

_____

_____

_____

_____

_____

_____

_____

3 Explaining people's actions

How could the following behaviour be explained?

a. A teenage boy has been very naughty, so his father doubles his pocket money.
b. A boy and girl are very much in love, so they decide to separate for six months.
c. A man idolizes a pop star. He dresses like him and behaves like him. Finally he shoots him dead.
d. A teenage boy and his father are in a car crash. The father dies, and the boy is seriously injured. Just as he is about to have an operation in the hospital, the surgeon says, 'I can't operate on this boy. He's my son.'

4 Deductions about the present and past

A detective is investigating a burglary at the home of Mr and Mrs Smith. Put in the correct modal verb of deduction.

'I wonder how the thief got in. He (a)

_____ used a ladder or he

(b) _____ had a key.
Ah! What's this? Broken glass by the kitchen door, and the door has been unlocked. He

(c) _____ broken the window, put his hand inside, and turned the key. That

(d) _____ made a noise. I wonder if the neighbours heard anything?'
(He goes next door to talk to the neighbours, and knocks on their door.)
'There's no reply. I suppose they

(e) _____ be on holiday, or they

(f) _____ watching television.'
(He listens at the letter-box.)
'I can hear voices. Someone

(g) _____ in. Rather odd.'
(He goes back to the Smiths' house.)
'Now, I wonder what was stolen. I don't think the Smith family is terribly well off, so the thief

(h) _____ found a lot to steal.
It was clever of him to come in just after Mrs Smith

went shopping. He (i) _____
known she would be out. What was that noise? It came

from upstairs. The burglar (j) _____

not _____ left the house yet! He

(k) _____ hiding upstairs! I'd better go and see.'

56

5 Letters to a problem page

Here are the replies that four people received to letters they had written to the Problem Page of a magazine.

Who do you think wrote each of them?
What was the writer's problem?
What can you guess about the people, their problems, and the other people in their lives?

You're obviously finding it very difficult to cope with your daughter at the moment - but remember it is during the teenage years that most parents wonder who should leave home, the child or the parents! You sound very sympathetic, even though you're not getting any sleep. If I were you, I'd say that midnight was certainly late enough for her to be out, both during the week and at the weekend, especially at her age. You didn't say whether your wife supports you in the ultimatum you've given your daughter. She should do – it sounds very reasonable to me.

The feelings you describe are very normal, especially when you are just about to take the enormous step of committing yourself to someone else for the rest of your life. Think long and hard about whether you want to be with this man for so long. His eating habits might seem unpleasant now, but what are you going to feel about them in twenty years' time? But don't wait too long! If what you say is true, you run the risk of losing him.

Regarding your other worry about this otherwise perfect man, there are many commercially available mouth-washes. Buy him some next time you're both doing the shopping!

A million other wives would like to know why this happens! It's a very common problem, and I don't have an answer. I can only say that many jobs in the house *can* be put off – they're not *that* urgent, even though you might think they are. If your main aim is to get things fixed, and not just to get *him* to do them, I think the answer is to learn some DIY skills yourself and then you can share out the tasks. It's not so difficult to saw wood and bang in nails. Another approach is to get involved in all the preparations for the job, hand over the tools, and help to clear up afterwards. I often think it's that part of the job that a man is actually putting off.

Girls your age do fall out with friends quite easily and regularly, so don't feel that this lonely state is going to last for ever! The first thing to get rid of is your self-pity. Only *you* can get yourself out of it. It's not your friends' fault that they have treated you in such a way, and it seems to me that you have to a certain extent deserved it. So think more positively, and ask your mum for some practical advice and loving support.

6 Multi-word verbs (1) – types 2 and 3

Match a multi-word verb in **A** with a definition from **B**. Is the multi-word verb type 2 or type 3? (Check the Grammar section on page 120.)

A

		Definition	Type
a.	to **talk over** a problem	= _____	___
b.	to **try out** an idea	= _____	___
c.	to **go off** a person/food	= _____	___
d.	to **call off** a meeting	= _____	___
e.	to **give up** smoking	= _____	___
f.	to **look into** a problem	= _____	___
g.	to **get over** an illness	= _____	___
h.	to **turn down** an offer	= _____	___
i.	to **look after** a child	= _____	___
j.	to **work out** a sum	= _____	___

B

1 to recover from
2 to experiment with
3 to cancel
4 to stop
5 to discuss
6 to care for
7 to not accept
8 to not like any more
9 to investigate
10 to solve

Put the pronoun **it** in the correct place in the following sentences.

a. Jan had a problem with her finances, so we talked

    _____ over _____, and now it's fine.

b. I had an idea for reorganizing the system. We tried

    _____ out _____, and it worked well.

c. I used to love ice cream, but since I found out how

    it's made, I've really gone _____ off _____.

d. We were due to have a meeting on Thursday, but

    we've had to call _____ off _____ because the chairperson's ill.

e. I wish you wouldn't smoke. Why don't you give

    _____ up _____?

f. I'm sorry to hear about your problem with the Tax

    Office. I promise I'll look _____ into _____ as soon as possible.

g. The best thing for backaches is rest. Don't worry.

    You'll soon get _____ over _____.

h. The job looks very attractive. You'd be a fool to

    turn _____ down _____.

i. That ring is extremely valuable. Make sure you

    look _____ after _____.

j. I need a calculator to see how much money I've got

    in my account. I can't work _____ out _____ in my head.

7 Forms of address

Richard Henderson is a doctor.

Elizabeth Henderson is a school-teacher.

Who would address him in the following way?

Who would address her in the following way?

sir	ma'am
mate	luv
old boy	dear
guv'nor	darling
Doctor	Elizabeth
Richard	Liz
Dick	Mummy
Daddy	Mum
Pop	Mom
Grandpa	Gran
Mr Henderson	Miss
Henderson	Mrs Henderson

UNIT 10

Expressing Habit

1 Adjectives of character

Match one of the following adjectives to each description.

**loyal   rude   lazy   dishonest   obstinate
big-headed   cheerful   unsociable   naive   moody**

a. _____ He thinks he's so wonderful. He's clever, but he knows it.

b. _____ One minute she's happy, and the next something will upset her and she won't speak to you for ages.

c. _____ He's always laughing and smiling. He's got a kind word to say to everyone.

d. _____ She's always telling lies, even when there's no need.

e. _____ He doesn't lift a finger in the house.

f. _____ She'd stand by you to the last, and would never say anything against you behind your back.

g. _____ He won't listen to anybody else's opinion. He's always got to be right.

h. _____ He's got absolutely no manners whatsoever.

i. _____ At parties he'll just sit in a corner, reading a book. It's not that he's shy, he just won't talk to anyone.

j. _____ If you told him the moon was made of green cheese, he'd believe you.

2 Present habit

Write similar sentences, using either the Present Simple, the Present Continuous (with **always**), or **will**, to illustrate the following characteristics.

He's very good company.

*He makes me laugh.
He's always telling jokes.
He'll not only tell funny stories, but he'll listen to what you've got to say as well.*

a. She's such an optimist.

_____

_____

b. He has terrible table manners.

_____

_____

c. He's so adventurous.

_____

_____

d. Our neighbours are really friendly.

_____

_____

e. My daughter is a bit naughty.

_____

f. But my son is so good-natured.

_____

g. She's a very outgoing person, isn't she?

_____

h. I wish you wouldn't be so fussy!

_____

i. He's painfully shy, isn't he?

_____

_____

3 Past habit

Write similar sentences, using either **used to** or **would**, to illustrate the following past habits.

My grandfather was such a kind man.
He used to know if something was wrong, and he'd always make it better.

a. Andrew could be very selfish at times.

_____

b. My sister was so untidy when she was young.

_____

c. My mother's big passion was walking.

_____

d. When he was younger, he was so spoilt.

_____

e. My parents were very interested in amateur theatricals.

_____

f. My English teacher had real favourites in the class.

_____

g. My mother was terribly house-proud.

_____

h. I was very sporty when I was a child.

_____

4 'Will' and 'would'

Both are used to express characteristic behaviour. If the speaker finds the behaviour annoying, **will** and **would** are stressed.

Compare the following:
My children are very good. On Saturday mornings they'll watch television and get their own breakfast so we can have a lie-in.
But they **will** fight about which one should feed the cat.

Re-write the following sentences, using **will** or **would**. If the sentences seem to express the speaker's annoyance, underline the modal verb to show that it is stressed.

a. My grandfather sat in his rocking chair for hours, watching the fire and sucking on his pipe.

_____

_____

b. My grandmother used to get very cross because he put his muddy boots on the table.

_____

_____

c. My dog is so intelligent. I don't have to tell her when it's time to go for a walk. She gets the lead and she tugs at my trousers until I stand up.

_____

_____

d. But she runs in other people's gardens and pulls up their flowers.

_____

_____

_____

e. When I was young, if we had a severe winter we were cut off for weeks on end, and we had to live on whatever was in the house.

_____

_____

_____

f. When my aunt, who's a bit deaf, wants some peace, she takes the batteries out of her hearing aid. It works! It's impossible to get through to her!

_____

_____

_____

g. But then she forgets where she put the batteries!

_____

_____

_____

h. My first boyfriend was an incurable romantic. He bought me flowers every Friday, and he wrote poems about us.

_____

_____

_____

5 Past Simple, 'used to', and 'would' for past habits

The following story is about Lucy Irvine, who went to live on a tropical island for a year with a man she refers to as G.

Which of the verbs in italics . . .

1 can change to **would** or **used to**?
2 can change only to **used to**?
3 must stay in the Past Simple?

Put (1), (2), or (3) in the spaces below.

Writer seeks wife for a year on tropical island

Lucy Irvine (a) *answered* this advertisement and made a dream come true. She (b) *went* to live on a tropical island from May 1981 to June 1982. The dream was more romantic than the reality. They took only a few provisions and so in order to survive, they fished and hunted for food. They (c) *lived* in a small tent, and at night they (d) *retired* quickly into it, otherwise they were attacked by all kinds of insects. Here they (e) *entertained* each other with stories of their childhood, but they (f) *argued* about how to organize their life on the island. Lucy (g) *liked* going for long walks, while G, who (h) *was* often ill, had to stay near their camp. Fresh water was a particular problem. There were few streams on the island, and the sun (i) *beat* down day after day, drying up fresh-water pools. They waited desperately for the rains to come; every day clouds (j) *formed* on the horizon and then they (k) *disappeared*. Their health suffered and they (l) *lost* a lot of weight. Any small cut or insect bite (m) *became* infected, and healed very slowly. At first they (n) *bathed* their wounds in the sea, but the salt water in fact made them worse.

Slowly their lives (o) *improved*. They learned to catch better fish, but they were never able to grow their own food. At the end of the year Lucy felt very sad to leave the island she had grown to love, but she knew it was time to go.

a ____   b ____   c ____   d ____   e ____

f ____   g ____   h ____   i ____   j ____

k ____   l ____   m ____   n ____   o ____

6 Gap filling

Here is an extract from Lucy Irvine's book, *Castaway*, in which she describes the year she spent on the tropical island called Tuin. In the extract she tells us how she organized the catching and preparation of food, as she and her companion were both suffering more and more from malnutrition. Fill each gap with one suitable word.

After a short time on Tuin, management and rationing of stores fell automatically into my hands. It followed

that I should (a) _____ over the cooking entirely as well. I worked to a system that was in fact extremely flexible, but guided by one or two

hard and fast principles (b) _____ made it into at least a partial routine. I believed in starting the day with something in our stomachs,

therefore (c) _____, however tiny the portions became, was absolutely regular. From time to time the position of the tide necessitated our going fishing the moment it was light

(d) _____ for us to see. We both found that our energy and enthusiasm on these dawn trips flagged very quickly if we went on a completely

(e) _____ stomach, and as we grew thinner, the mild morning cool seemed to bite right into our bones, weakening and demoralizing us. So even if it meant stumbling around in the dark, I

(f) _____ sure that the least we had was half a mug of hot tea inside us

(g) _____ we went. The mere heat and ritual of this seemed to improve our spirits, for

there cannot be (h) _____ energy value in sugarless black tea.
The time and content of the next meal of the day

(i) _____ entirely on our luck fishing. If, for instance, we caught shark or a big queenfish or tuna in the morning, we would have

enough for a lunch and a (j) _____. I would poach a couple of steaks at midday and preserve another two servings by

(k) _____ salt and vinegar over the pieces of fish, which were then left in the shade, to be cooked later on. As the weather

(l) _____ hotter, we could not risk keeping the fish even a few hours,

(m) _____ we either dried what was left over or used it for bait. If we had no luck at

all with fishing, we would (n) _____ to camp for a rest and a cup of tea in the shade, and then transfer our attentions to gathering the main ingredients for a meal from the beaches.

7 'Get' versus 'be'

Compare the following sentences.

Don't worry. You'll soon **get used** to living in a hot climate.
I'm not **used** to such hard work.

Be describes a state; **get** expresses a change of state.

Complete the sentences with either **be** or **get** in the correct form, and one of the following.

used	**married**	**divorced**	**ready**
better	**to know**	**lost**	

a. When Brian became famous, he had to

_____ to being followed everywhere by journalists. He didn't like it at all.
b. A Is Kate still married?

   B No, she _____ last year. She was given custody of the children.

c. When are you _____? Can I come
to the wedding?

d. If I were you I'd take a map. You never know, you

might _____.

e. Excuse me! Could you tell us how to get to Derby?

We _____, and we haven't a clue
where we are.

f. **A** Where's your mother?

B In the bathroom. She _____ to
go out.

A I know. We're going to a party, and if she
doesn't hurry up we'll be late. I don't know

what takes her so long. I _____
since seven o'clock.

g. **A** How are you feeling?

B I _____ slowly, but I still feel a
bit weak.

h. When we had our first child, I found it quite

difficult. I _____ not

_____ to being woken up in the
middle of the night. We've got five now, so I

_____ to it!

i. My first impressions of Jenny were not very

favourable, but as I _____

_____ her, I realized what a lovely
person she was.

j. If you _____ to hot, spicy food, I
don't suggest you try this dish. There's a lot of
chilli in it.

k. _____ is a painful experience for a
husband and a wife, but it is much more painful for
the children, if they have any.

l. **A** How's your wife's back these days?

B It _____ now, thanks.

8 Words with similar meanings

Which words on the left-hand side can combine with a
word on the right-hand side? Draw arrows to link the
words in each box.

a.

	time
	food
to waste	money
to spend	energy
	an opportunity
	paper

b.

	person
	behaviour
strange	country
odd	number
	socks
	man out
	jobs

c.

	face
	cold
	sense
common	knowledge
plain	clothes
	paper
	food

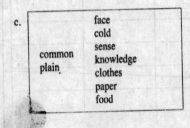

d.

	nose
	mistake
	decision
big	man
great	writer
	building
	friend

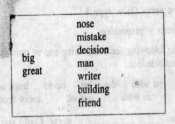

e.

	car
	meal
	worker
fast	temper
quick	lane of a motorway
	food restaurant

9 Synonyms and antonyms

Think of a synonym, or a near synonym, and an antonym for the following adjectives. Sometimes several words are possible.

Adjective	Synonym	Antonym
mad	insane, crazy	sane, sensible
huge		
chatty		
keen		
genuine		
essential		
powerful		
simple		
deceitful		
fair (decision)		
kind		
conceited		
brave		
loyal (friend)		
plain		

10 Multi-word verbs (2) – type 4

Verb + adverb + preposition

Complete the following sentences using one of the following combinations.

away with   **on with**   **down on**   **up to**   **back on**
up against   **in with**   **out of**   **away from**

a. We've run _____ sugar. Could you buy some more?

b. Please don't let me disturb you. Carry

_____ your work.

c. We must try to cut _____ the amount of money we spend. We just can't make ends meet.

d. Keep _____ me! I've got a terrible cold, and I don't want to give it to you.

e. When I look _____ my childhood, I realize what a happy time it was.

f. She's such a snob. She looks _____ people who have to work for their living.

g. The only people she looks _____ are her grandparents.

h. Children grow _____ their clothes so quickly. It costs a fortune to clothe them properly.

i. The government have come _____ a big problem in their economic policy. The unions won't co-operate, and management doesn't approve of what they're trying to do.

j. Face _____ the facts, Joey, and stop living with your head in the clouds. You'll never get anywhere if you don't work at it.

k. The antique table is very beautiful, but it doesn't fit

_____ the rest of the furniture, which is modern.

l. He tries to get _____ doing nothing around the house by charming everyone, but they've all learnt his tricks.

UNIT 11

Hypothesis

1 Should have done / should have been doing / shouldn't have done

Write two sentences, one in the positive and one in the negative, for each of the following situations.

Margaret was mugged last night. She was walking home alone.
She shouldn't have been walking home alone.
She should have gone with someone or taken a taxi.

a. Andrew was arrested last night. He was driving home after a party, and he'd had too much to drink.

_____

_____

_____

b. Graham was wounded when he tried to stop a man robbing a post office. The robber shot him in the leg.

_____

_____

_____

c. Annie lost her purse yesterday. It was in her bag, but her bag wasn't fastened, and she left it unattended for a few minutes while she bought a newspaper.

_____

_____

_____

d. My briefcase was stolen from my car yesterday. I'd left it lying on the passenger seat while I popped out to do some shopping, and I'm afraid the window had been left open.

_____

_____

_____

e. Jenny was caught travelling on a train without a ticket.

_____

_____

_____

f. There was a fire at Henry's house yesterday. Their son Max was playing with matches, and he set fire to the furniture. Unfortunately the flat wasn't insured, so they've lost everything.

_____

_____

_____

2 Third-conditional sentences

Look at the pictures and write some third-conditional sentences.

If the man had been looking where he was going, instead of reading a newspaper, he'd have seen the dog and wouldn't have tripped over it. If he hadn't been looking . . .

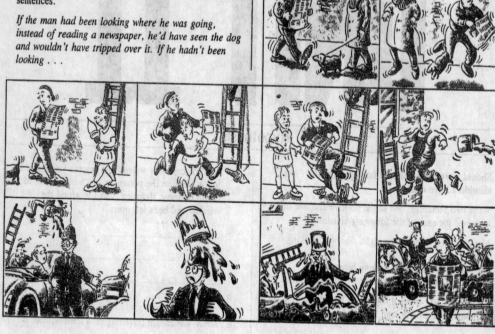

3 Conditionals: first, second, third, and zero

Put the verbs in brackets in the correct forms. There are examples of first, second and third conditionals, and the zero conditional as well.

a. If you _____ (go) away, you

_____ (write) to me, won't you?

b. Unless house plants _____ (water)

regularly, they _____ (die) quite
quickly.

c. What noisy neighbours you've got! If mine

_____ (be) as bad as yours, I

_____ (go) crazy!

d. You're late again! If you _____ (be)

late again tomorrow, your pay _____
(stop)!

e. The passengers at the front of the plane were all
killed, but Alice, who was sitting at the back,

survived. If she _____ (sit) nearer

the front, she _____ (kill).

f. I eat meat once or twice a day, but I

_____ (not like) it if it

_____ (undercook).

g. Eat your soup. If you _____ (not

hurry) up, it _____ (get) cold.

h. There are mice in your kitchen. If you

_____ (have) a cat, the mice

_____ (disappear) immediately.

i. The style of that dress is lovely, but I'm not so keen

on the colour. If the blue _____ (be)

a bit lighter, it _____ (look) better.

j. A We're penniless. Did you know that?
    B It's because our holiday cost so much. You
       should have listened to me. If we

    _____ (go) where I wanted to

    go, it _____ (be) a lot cheaper

    And we _____ (have) some
    money in the bank now.

k. She was badly hurt when the car in which she was a passenger hit another car. If she

_____ (wear) her seat belt, she

_____ (not hurt) so badly.

l. Give me that message for Peter. If I

_____ (see) him this afternoon, I

_____ (give) it to him.

m. Mmm! This meal's delicious! If I

_____ (can) cook as well as this, I

_____ (open) a restaurant.

n. My wife and I met on a cruise. I was on it because I was recovering from an illness, and she was the

ship's doctor. Just think! If I _____

(not be) ill, and if she _____ (not be)

the doctor, we _____ (not meet), we

_____ (not get) married, and our

children _____ (not be) born! What a thought!

o. If you _____ (be able) to do this

exercise, you _____ (be) very clever!

4 I wish . . .

Write a sentence using I wish . . . for each of the following situations.

We've come on holiday to Westby and I'm hating it. *I wish we hadn't come here.*

a. The weather's horrible.

b. We can't go swimming.

c. Last night we went to the Ritz restaurant, and I was ill all night.

d. There's nothing to do in the evening.

e. We haven't got a television in our hotel room.

f. I wanted to go to Spain.

g. But the rest of my family persuaded me to come to Westby.

h. The children keep asking me for money.

i. My wife says it's her holiday too, and she won't help with the children.

j. In the hotel, we have to get up for breakfast at 7.00 in the morning.

5 Wishes and regrets

Read the text.

'I live in a squalid flat. I'm out of work and on the dole. I didn't have a good education; in fact I left school at fifteen without any qualifications. I wrote about fifty job applications and didn't get a single job. I went for a lot of interviews, but I don't really know how to behave at interviews, I can't answer their questions very well.

I sit about at home every day, watching TV, and smoking. I get through about forty cigarettes a day, so I don't have enough money to go to football matches any more. A friend of mine from school has got a job at a travel agent's. He travels all over the world for his holidays, and he's always telling me about wonderful trips to Spain and Greece. I've never been abroad! I'm so depressed. I think the worst thing is having nothing to look forward to. I'm nineteen, and I have a lifetime of nothing in front of me.'

Write sentences based on the text, using **He wishes**
. . . **He should have** . . . and the second and third
conditionals.

He wishes he lived somewhere nicer.
He should have stayed at school.
If he had a job, he'd be happier.

_____

_____

_____

_____

_____

_____

_____

_____

_____

6 Idioms

Here is a list of idioms. Decide what you think is the
key word, then look in your dictionary to see if you
are right. Re-write the sentences in non-idiomatic
English.

We're a team, and we have to work together, but I
don't think Bill is **pulling his weight.**

Key word: **pull**

I don't think Bill is doing his fair share of the work.

a. The bank had installed video monitoring equipment,
   so the robber was **caught red-handed.**

   _____

   _____

   _____

b. All negotiations in the miners' pay dispute had
   broken down, and the strike was due to start next
   day. Then, **at the eleventh hour**, the management
   made a new offer.

   _____

   _____

c. The prisoner left the prison, having served his
   sentence. He was a reformed character, determined
   to turn over a new leaf.

   _____

   _____

d. Setting up your own business should be quite a
   simple affair, but there is so much **red tape**
   involved, with tax offices, local government offices,
   planning permission offices and so on, that it can
   take years.

   _____

   _____

e. My father agreed to lend me his car for the
   evening, but when I asked for some money for
   petrol, he **put his foot down.**

   _____

   _____

f. 'I know the hotel isn't wonderful, and yes, the
   weather isn't great, but we're all on holiday, so
   let's **make the most of it** and try to have a good
   time, shall we?'

   _____

   _____

g. **A** The question is, who left the window open?
   B For goodness' sake, John. Stop **splitting hairs!** It doesn't matter who left the window open. The fact is that someone did, and that's how the budgie escaped.

   _____
   _____
   _____

h. He stole money from his wife's purse so that he could go out drinking. But she **got her own back** by locking him out, so he had to sleep in the garden that night.

   _____
   _____
   _____

i. Don't worry about Josephine. She shouts a lot, but really she doesn't mean it. Her **bark is worse than her bite.**

   _____
   _____
   _____

i. **A** My wife and I just can't control our finances. No matter how hard we try, we're always overdrawn at the end of the month.
   B Jack and I are **in the same boat.** I think it must be the cost of living that has gone up.

   _____
   _____
   _____

7 Verb + object + preposition

Put the correct preposition into each gap.

a. He invested all his money _____ stocks and shares.

b. Could you throw that book _____ me, please? I'd like to have a quick look at it.

c. You horrible child! If you throw stones

   _____ my dog again, I'll smack your bottom.

d. I accused him _____ cheating at cards, but he denied it.

e. He congratulated her _____ passing her driving test.

f. The weather prevented the boat _____ sailing across the Atlantic.

g. They thanked him _____ being so kind.

h. She ultimately forgave me _____ crashing her car, but she never forgot it.

i. They invited us _____ their wedding, but we couldn't go.

j. I warned him _____ the dangers of driving without a seat belt.

k. I prefer living in town _____ living in the suburbs.

l. They provided me _____ food and a bed, which was very kind.

m. The smell of the food reminded me _____ when I was a child.

n. He spent all his money _____ fast cars and gambling.

o. She stopped him _____ driving home by hiding the car keys.

UNIT 12

Articles

1 Gap filling

Put a, the or nothing into each gap.

Lovesick teenager
snatched from cliff

(a) _____ lovesick teenager, threatening to jump seventy

feet from (b) _____ cliffs at (c) _____ seaside resort,

was saved by (d) _____ human chain of (e) _____
policemen today.

(f) _____ eighteen-year old had driven from his home

in (g) _____ Lake District to Langhorn, near (h) _____
Bournemouth, to talk his girlfriend out of breaking off
their three-month romance.

He threatened to jump off (i) _____ balcony at her

house, but when she dialled (j) _____ 999 he dashed to

(k) _____ edge of (l) _____ cliffs below (m) _____
Metropole Hotel.

(n) _____ police found him sitting on (o) _____ edge.

They chatted to him for twenty minutes in (p) _____
darkness, then clung together and grabbed him.

He was later released after (q) _____ treatment by

(r) _____ hospital doctor.

(s) _____ police spokesman said, 'There was (t) _____
high wind, it was pitch dark at about 2 a.m., and

(u) _____ grass on (v) _____ cliff top was wet and

slippery. It was (w) _____ brave rescue.

'It was (x) _____ case of (y) _____ unrequited love. The
youngster was upset after his romance broke up, but he
has now recovered his senses.'

2 Expressions with or without articles (1)

Underline the correct version in each sentence.

I've got some cigarettes but I haven't got light / a light.
Light / the light travels faster than sound / the sound.

a. We're having lamb / the lamb for lunch.
b. The sheep gave birth to lamb / a lamb in the
   middle of the night.
c. Would you like cake / a cake?
d. No, thanks. I don't like cake / a cake.
e. This suit is made of very fine cloth / the very fine
   cloth.
f. Can you get cloth / a cloth, please? I've just spilt
   tea / a tea on your carpet.
g. I went to a talk / talk on Russian revolution / the
   Russian revolution last night. It was very
   interesting.
h. There has been a talk / talk of redundancies at the
   British Shipping Company.
i. Service / a service in restaurants isn't as good as it
   used to be.
j. The Health Service / Health Service is suffering
   from severe cutbacks.
k. The Times / Times is one of Britain's oldest
   newspapers.
l. Time / the time and tide / the tide wait for no
   man. (proverb)
m. I don't usually like poetry / the poetry.
n. But here's a poem / poem I do like.
o. Do you want an ice / ice in your whisky?
p. Ice / the ice at the North and South Poles is said to
   be melting little by little.

3 Expressions with or without articles (2)

Put a, the or nothing into each gap.

a. Excuse me. Is there _____ post office near
   here?
b. A We haven't got any money.

   B It's all right. I'm going to _____ bank.

c. My wife and I went out for _____ meal last

night. _____ food was excellent. I don't

usually like _____ Chinese food, but

_____ duck was superb.

d. When she looked behind her, she saw _____

strange man following her.

e. Has _____ postman been yet? I'm expecting

_____ parcel.

f. We've moved to _____ lovely house in

_____ country. It's got _____ views of

fields and hills, and there's _____ garden at

_____ back.

g. Do you want to speak to Jack? I'll just go and get

him. He's in _____ garden.

h. _____ government without _____ strong

leader will not produce _____ good policies.

i. _____ government has introduced _____

law to ban _____ sale of _____ air guns

to _____ people under _____ age of eighteen.

j. My brother joined _____ Army because he

likes playing with _____ guns. .

4 Correcting mistakes of articles

Correct the mistakes in the following sentences.

a. Jane, has anyone ever told you that you've got
   some lovely fingers?
b. I'm very interested in the history, especially the
   history of Western Europe.
c. What a lovely weather we're having! It's such a
   nice day!
d. We're trying to sell our house. People came to see
   it on Saturday, and they were quite interested, but
   some people who saw it on Sunday morning were
   very rude and said they didn't like it at all.
e. Did you remember to buy a bread while you were
   out at some shops?
f. Crossing the English Channel can be quite
   unpleasant in the bad weather.
g. People who live on the floor above ours work in a
   government ministry.
h. What's the government going to do about the
   unemployment?

5 Numerical expressions with the indefinite article

Write a sentence using a numerical expression with
a/an.

twice a day; £1.50 a metre.

Sales Representative
for Computer Company

Based in London
£15,000 p.a.

Albion Electronics
171 Queens Road
London SW2

POTATOES
10p Lb.

30 mph

PILLS
One to be
taken every
8 hours.

SINGLE ROOM
with Shower,
£20·00

20 KINGS
20

£2·50/
METRE

** £1·90
** Gallon

**Flights to New York
Departure times:**

6.30, 10.15, 12.45,
15.20, 17.05.

6 Expressions with or without articles (3)

There are many expressions with either **a, the** or no article. Put **a, the** or nothing into each gap.

a. In my job, I do _____ business with people from all over the world.

b. I'm going to do _____ shopping. Do you want anything?

c. I was late for _____ work this morning.

d. Can you keep _____ secret? I'm getting married.

e. He got _____ sack because he was caught stealing money.

f. It isn't easy, but I think we're making _____ progress.

g. I lost _____ control of the car and crashed into a wall.

h. Make _____ love, not _____ war.

i. If you make _____ promise, you must keep it.

j. When buying a house, you should take into

_____ consideration how near it is to public transport.

k. He set _____ fire to his factory so that he could claim the insurance.

l. You must make _____ effort to get to know your neighbours.

m. I've been to all the countries of Europe with

_____ exception of Albania.

n. If you're in Paris, take _____ opportunity to visit the Louvre.

7 Nouns from multi-word verbs

The noun formed from a multi-word verb sometimes has the same meaning as the verb, and sometimes not.

The **rain poured down**.

There was a sudden **downpour**, and we all got soaked. } (the same)

He **fell down** the stairs and hurt his leg. } (not the same:
Drink was her **downfall**. } **a downfall** means **ruin**)

Look at the following pairs of sentences, and decide if the noun and the verb express the same meaning or not. Notice that the particle can sometimes come before the verb.

a. I was **brought up** by my parents to be a strict Catholic.
I had a traditional **upbringing**, but a happy one. My family was very close.

_____

b. The Government is **going ahead** with its plans to denationalize the coal industry.
We can't start work on the extension to our house until we get the **go-ahead** from the local Council.

_____

c. He **came out** of the room and walked slowly down the corridor.
The **outcome** of the election is that the Conservative Party has a majority of ninety in the House of Commons.

_____

d. He **looked out** of the window to see what the weather was like.
Here is the weather forecast. The **outlook** for tomorrow is quite good. It should stay fine all day long.

_____

e. Thieves **broke through** a wall to get to the safe.
There has been a significant **breakthrough** in the search to find a cure for the common cold.

_____

f. The group made several hit records, but **broke up** so that they could pursue their careers alone.
He's been terribly upset since the **break-up** of his marriage.

_____

g. I **drew back** the curtains and let the sunshine in.
Yours is an interesting plan, but I'm afraid it has two **drawbacks**. It would be too expensive, and it would take too long to build.

_____

h. She **cried out** in her sleep. She must have been having a bad dream.
There was a public **outcry** when it was proposed to close the National Health Service.

_____

Match the nouns from phrasal verbs (a–h on page 72) with the following synonyms or definitions.

result   *outcome*

i. permission to continue   _____

j. what seems likely to happen; prospect _____

k. disadvantage   _____

l. childhood training   _____

m. protest   _____

n. significant development or discovery _____

o. separation; disintegration   _____

8 Vocabulary: nationality words

Complete the chart. Notice that the adjective is not always the same as the word for a person.

Country	Adjective	A person	The nation
Mexico	Mexican	A Mexican	The Mexicans
Denmark	Danish	A Dane	The Danes
Greece			
Italy			
Poland			
Sweden			
Spain			
Belgium			
Brazil			
Russia			
Scotland			
Turkey			
China			
Japan			
Switzerland			

Do the same for the following countries. Notice that in this group we cannot say * a French, an English. Add a suitable noun, such as **student, girl, doctor, businessman**.

Country	Adjective	A person	The nation
England	English	An English lawyer	The English
France			
Wales			
Ireland			
Holland			

9 Fixed expressions + preposition

Put the correct preposition or combination of prepositions into each gap.

a. After running up the stairs he was

_____ breath.

b. My sister and I are very different. We don't have

much _____ common at all.

c. I don't want to go to Franco's Restaurant again.
We always go there. Let's go somewhere else

_____ a change.

d. I don't dislike Jane. _____ the
contrary, I'm very fond of her.

e. _____ general I go abroad for my
holidays, but occasionally I stay at home.

f. It always pays to buy high-quality goods.

_____ the long run it's cheaper.

g. You most certainly cannot borrow my car. It's

completely _____ the question.

h. This is a very important decision. All our lives are

_____ stake.

i. I went on holiday _____ my own

because sometimes I like being _____
myself.

j. I'll do it tomorrow. No, _____
second thoughts, I'll do it today.

REVISION 3

1 In the following article there are twenty gaps. After some gaps there is a verb in brackets. Put the verb in the correct tense.

Yesterday I _____ went _____ (go) to the park.

When there is no verb in brackets, put in one suitable word — perhaps a preposition, a modal verb, an article, etc.

The sun rises in _____ the _____ east.

NEIGHBOURS

'Good walls make good neighbours' is an extremely negative way of viewing the people

(a) _____ live next door. We all have neighbours, and it makes life so much easier if

you can manage to (b) _____ on well with them.
In Britain, over 30,000 people

(c) _____ year complain about noisy neighbours — their music, parties, pets, children, and cars, in that order, and many of these complaints go to court. One lawyer estimated that every solicitor

in the country (d) _____ handle at least ten cases of disputes between neighbours a year.
Take the case of Peter Knowles and his wife, Pat. They were sitting in their garden when a cricket ball came flying over the wall, narrowly

(e) _____ (miss) Pat. Peter was

furious. 'If it (f) _____ (hit) her,

it (g) _____ have killed her.' He

went to court, and won (h) _____ case, to stop his neighbours' children playing cricket in

their garden. This was just one incident in the feud between the Knowles family and their neighbours, the Cunninghams. Ken Cunningham

(i) _____ to park his car outside his own home, until one day Peter put a brick through the windscreen. Peter was convinced that that was *his* parking space. 'I didn't know I was parking in his

space,' said Ken. 'He (j) _____

have spoken to me instead (k) _____ smashing my car.'
The case ended up in court again, and both parties

(l) _____ (order) to keep the peace; but the war still goes

(m) _____. 'If we

(n) _____ afford it, we

(o) _____ move,' said Ken, 'but we can't. And anyway, we like it here, apart from old fusspot next door. I wish he

(p) _____ learn that being good neighbours is a matter of give and take.'
All was not easy between the occupants of numbers 37 and 39, Johnson's Walk, Bolton. Mr and Mrs Brown are a retired couple, and live at number 37. The previous occupier of number 39 was an old lady. 'She was very quiet,' said Mrs Janet Brown. 'We never

(q) _____ to hear anything.' Then the Smiths moved in with their eight children. 'The first night they were in, they had a party. The noise

was unbelievable. They (r) _____ have had at least forty people, all dancing and singing.' They complained bitterly to the neighbours. Mrs Smith said, 'I wish she (s) _____ (tell) us we were making a lot of noise. We would have invited them round! We don't really make much noise,

it's just that they aren't (t) _____
to having children living next door.'
So what are the golden rules for harmony between
neighbours? Sympathy, tolerance, and honesty. Don't
think that they're making a noise just to annoy you,
and don't go round when you're in a fury. Calm down
first — then just try to be adult!

2 Choose the best answer, **A**, **B**, **C** or **D**.

a. He said I hadn't given him his book back, but I

was _____ sure I had.
A entirely   **B** totally   **C** quite   **D** rather

b. There was an accident on the motorway, and we

were _____ for over an hour.
A held down   **B** held up   **C** put back   **D** put up

c. I'll see you outside the cinema. Make sure you're

_____. I don't want to miss the
beginning of the film.
A at times   **B** in time   **C** before time   **D** on time

d. The winner of the competition was

_____ with a cheque for £5,000.
A presented   **B** given   **C** awarded   **D** offered

e. I really need your help, so don't

_____, please.
A let me through   **B** let me in   **C** let me off
D let me down

f. He was homesick, and _____ all his
friends and family.
A missed   **B** lost   **C** lacked   **D** desired

g. The receptionist _____ me where to
find my room.
A explained   **B** told   **C** said   **D** directed

h. If the radio isn't working properly, you should

_____ to the shop. You've only just
bought it.
A take it back   **B** take it out   **C** bring it back
D bring it up

i. You'll fail the exam _____ you start
revising.
A if   **B** until   **C** when   **D** unless

j. Employees hope that their salary will

_____ with the cost of living.
A raise   **B** rise   **C** grow   **D** increase

k. It took me a long time to _____ the
disappointment of losing the match.
A get through   **B** get off   **C** get over
D get down

l. I turned down the job, _____ the
attractive salary.
A because   **B** because of   **C** despite
D although

m. I met my husband _____ I was at
university.
A until   **B** during   **C** since   **D** while

n. The doctor _____ me to spend a
few days in bed.
A suggested   **B** proposed   **C** advised   **D** made

o. I looked everywhere for some cooking oil, but I

could only find _____.
A a little   **B** little   **C** a few   **D** few

p. I wanted to build a bookcase, but I couldn't make

_____ of the instructions.
A understanding   **B** sense   **C** reality   **D** sight

q. He failed the test many times. _____,
he didn't stop trying.
A But   **B** So   **C** Although   **D** However

r. It was such a funny sight that we couldn't stop

_____
A laughing   **B** to laughing   **C** laugh
D to laugh

s. We didn't have a very nice holiday. The weather

was _____ awful.
A completely   **B** totally   **C** absolutely
D terribly

t. _____ the people who saw the
exhibition thought it was marvellous.
A Most   **B** All   **C** Every one   **D** Each

u. If you _____ careful with electricity,
you might get a shock.
A don't   **B** won't   **C** wouldn't   **D** aren't

v. My purse is _____ in the kitchen,
but I'm not quite sure where.
A nowhere   **B** anywhere   **C** somewhere
D everywhere

w. When he _____ all the letters, he
took them to the post office.
A had been writing   **B** had written   **C** wrote
D has written

x. If I breathe in, I get a sharp _____ in my chest.
A hurt   B wound   C ache   D pain

y. Thank you for the invitation. What time would you like _____?
A we come   B we to come   C us to come   D that we come

z. If I _____ the trick with my own eyes, I would never have believed it possible.
A hadn't been seeing   B hadn't seen   C didn't see   D wouldn't have seen

3 Finish each of the following sentences in such a way that it means exactly the same as the original sentence.

I'm sure she's French.
She must *be French.*

a. I think you should cut down on your spending.

I suggest _____

b. I'm sorry you didn't tell me that I'd upset you.

I wish _____

c. It's possible that your car was stolen.

Your car _____

d. You're supposed to be working. Why aren't you?

You should _____

e. He's finding it easier to work at night.

He's getting _____

f. 'I'm sorry I was late,' he said.

He apologized _____

g. I haven't seen this film before.

This is _____

h. Peter can run faster than me.

I can't _____

i. 'Have you done this sort of work before?' she asked me.

She asked me if _____

j. I'm sure she didn't do it on purpose.

She can't _____

4 The word in brackets at the end of each of the following sentences can be used to form a word that fits suitably in the gap. Fill each gap in this way.

My car isn't very _____*reliable*_____. It's always letting me down. (rely)

a. I wrote _____ letters of application, but got no reply. (end)

b. I apologize for the mistake made by my office. There appears to have been a slight

_____. (understand)

c. Burning coal is an _____ way of heating a house. Gas is much cheaper. (economy)

d. I've just been told some _____ news. (astonish)

e. In _____ with most other countries, Britain has a very high rate of heart attacks. (compare)

f. We have to keep our costs as small as possible. We have so many _____ trying to take our customers away. (compete)

g. There are very few _____ places left on earth. Man has been nearly everywhere. (explore)

h. There is extreme _____ in many Third World countries. (poor)

i. I recommend the _____ of the house. It's delicious. (special)

j. He was dismissed for _____. He lost the order of a very important customer. (care)

5 Make all the changes and additions necessary to produce, from the following eight sets of words and phrases, eight sentences which together make a complete letter. Note carefully from the example what kind of alterations need to be made.

I / be / very pleased / hear your good news.
I was very pleased to hear your good news.

Dear Suzanna,

a. Thank you / your letter / arrive / yesterday.

_____

b. As / I be sure / you / imagine / we / be / very busy recently, / having just / move / into / new house.

_____

_____

c. We / slowly / settle / in /, although it / be / a long time before everything / finish.

_____

_____

77

d. Jack / put down / the living room carpet at the moment /, and tonight we / have / house-warming party.

_____

_____

e. I / be / sorry / hear you / not / come. / If we / tell you / earlier, you / can / put off your mother's visit.

_____

_____

f. You say / your letter / you / like / visit us / summer.

_____

_____

g. I / be / sure / we / finish / all the things / we / want / do / house / then.

_____

_____

h. We / see / exactly / kind of carpet / we want / put upstairs, / and we / buy / it tomorrow.

_____

_____

Keep in touch. Give our regards to David.

Love

Mary

6 Put the correct preposition or adverb into each gap.

a. He asked the children to put _____ their toys _____ once.

b. When you grow _____, you can go _____ by yourself _____ night, but not before.

c. Come _____! Put your coat _____, and let's go _____ for a walk.

d. He was accused _____ stealing a thousand pounds _____ his employer.

e. I'm thinking _____ going to Australia to work _____ a sheep farm.

f. Don't talk _____ her. She's _____ a bad mood.

g. I suffer _____ headaches, especially _____ the evening.

h. He died _____ a heart attack _____ a very early age. He was only _____ his early forties.

i. Please let me get _____ with my work; it has to be finished _____ 3.00.

j. The dentist pulled _____ one of my back teeth.

k. Smoking is bad _____ your health. You should try to cut down _____ the amount you smoke, or better still, you should give _____.

l. I came _____ some old pictures of me _____ school while I was tidying _____ my drawers.

m. Lean the ladder carefully _____ the wall. Otherwise it will fall _____.

n. I have very little _____ common _____ him. We don't have much to talk _____.

o. I stayed _____ all night listening _____ records.

p. I've saved _____ enough money _____ us to live _____ the interest _____ the rest _____ our lives.

q. If you aren't satisfied _____ our products, bring them _____ to the shop and we will give you your money _____

He was walking _____ the field

_____ his child _____ his back.

He had to pay _____ the damage he had

done _____ my car.

It's very difficult to get _____ touch

_____ my sister, because she isn't

_____ the telephone.

In each of the following sentences there is one spelling
mistake. Find it and write the word correctly in the
space provided.

a. Ambassadors from several counties have been trying

   to find a peaceful solution to the conflict._____

b. My wife and I decided to go on a Mediterranean
   cruise to celebrate our fifteenth wedding

   anniversery._____

c. Psychologists tell us that children need their

   parents to be consistant._____

d. Having traveled widely throughout the whole world,
   she spoke many foreign languages, including

   Portuguese and Czech. _____

e. We paid insufficient attention to finding adequate
   accomodation, with the result that we had nowhere

   to stay. _____

f. We thought we had made detailed arrangements for
   the journey, but as soon as we set off we realized

   we had not planed enough. _____

g. My interest in currant affairs only goes as far as the

   football results._____

h. We crossed over the bridge, past by St Paul's
   Cathedral, and proceeded home via the shortest

   possible route. _____

i. The beach looked very attractive, but I had to miss
   the opportunity to go swimming as I had not

   brought my batheing costume. _____

j. Our neighbours interfere with our enjoyment of the
   weekend by their constant quarreling and noisy

   relatives._____

k. My cousin tried to be helpfull, but in fact he only

   succeeded in making matters worse._____

l. Young children should not be allow to play with

   knives, or any other dangerous instruments._____

m. To be a proficient piano player needs a lot of
   practise, and ideally one should have a teacher from

   the beginning. _____

n. He had been sufferring terribly, and it was no

   surprise when we heard he had died._____

8 In the following dialogues, mark where the main stress
is in B's replies. Use a coloured pen.

A I thought you didn't like cake.
B I a<u>dore</u> cake.

a. A It's about time you took your library books
      back.
   B I did take them back.

b. A Who took my library book back? I hadn't
      finished it.
   B I took it back.

c. A Did you know that John and Mary are coming
      tonight?
   B I knew John was coming.

d. A John and Mary are coming tonight. Did you
      know that?
   B I knew that ages ago.

e. A You haven't been shopping, have you? I did it
      all this morning.
   B I wish you'd told me.

f. A I think Peter wanted you to give him the
      information.
   B You should have told him.

g. A When is your wife going to New York?
   B She's in New York.

h. A Is your wife in Los Angeles?
   B She's in New York.

i. A Who told Anne that I'd lost her dog?
   B I didn't tell her.

j. A I wish you hadn't told Anne about her dog.
   B I didn't tell her.

k. A When are you going to mow the lawn?
   B I'm going to do it soon.

l. A Have you mowed the lawn yet?
   B No, but I'm going to.

m. A Are you a nervous flier or not?
   B I've never been in a plane.

n. A She's got four daughters and three cats.
   B She's got four sons and three cats.

o. A She's got four daughters and three cats.
   B She's got three daughters and one cat.

INITIAL TEST

Question 1

a. at
b. on
c. to learn
d. Their
e. for
f. since
g. who
h. are
i. other
j. in Mrs Stoppard's class
k. has
l. as
m. an earlier train
n. does
o. would be
p. there is
q. said
r. what people are interested in
s. ask
t. will start

Question 2

a. lend
b. earns
c. journey
d. cost
e. bring
f. game
g. fell
h. telling
i. waste
j. room

Question 3

a. When did they arrive?
b. How long did he stay at the hotel?
c. What are you thinking about?
d. How many daughters has he got?
e. Where do they usually have lunch?
f. How often do you go abroad?
g. How long have you worked here?
h. What does 'to chop' mean?
i. What sort of soup would you like?
j. Who discovered America?

Question 4

Sample answers

a. Excuse me! Could you tell me where there is a bank?
b. Five tens and the rest in fives, please.
c. I'm afraid I haven't got the money today, but I can pay you tomorrow.
d. Excuse me! I asked for a black coffee.
e. Could I have a look at your newspaper?
f. I'm having a party at my house on Saturday. Would you like to come?
g. That's very kind of you, but I'm afraid I can't make it.
h. Can you change this for me?
i. Well, it's summer there at the moment, and it gets very hot, so take clothes that will keep you cool.
j. Could you recommend a good English dictionary for me, please?

UNIT 1

Exercise 1

1 j. Present Simple
2 g. Present Perfect Continuous
3 h. Present Perfect Simple
4 e. Past Simple passive
5 a. Present Continuous
6 f. Present Continuous passive
7 b. Past Simple
8 d. Past Continuous
9 i. Present Perfect passive
10 c. Present Simple passive

Exercise 2

a. was kidnapped
b. has been released
c. was examined
d. is said
e. was found
f. saw
g. contacted
h. was told
i. has been found
j. is being questioned

Exercise 3

a. You will be given your tickets at the airport.
b. I was asked a lot of questions about my background.
c. Airline passengers are usually shown how to use a life jacket at the beginning of the flight.
d. If you are offered a cheap camera, don't buy it.
e. He has been given six months to live.
f. You will be told what you have to do when you arrive.
g. I was advised by my parents to spend some time abroad before looking for work.
h. I have been told a lot about you.
i. At interviews, you are asked quite searching questions.
j. In a few years' time I will be sent to our New York office.

Exercise 4

a. What do you think
   What are you thinking
b. I'm expecting
   I expect
c. He appears
   Roy Pond is appearing
d. Something smells
   Why are you smelling
e. the meat weighs
   Why are you weighing
f. I see
   She's seeing
g. I'm having
   He has
h. It looks
   Are you looking
i. You're guessing
   I guess
j. What are you thinking
   How much do you think

Exercise 5

Sample answers

a. since
b. use, operation
c. involved
d. more
e. improving
f. human
g. are
h. accuracy
i. so
j. part, role
k. make
l. mistakes, errors
m. back
n. ever
o. replaced

Exercise 7

1 e   2 c   3 a
4 d   5 b   6 f

Exercise 8

a. for . . . in
b. on
c. with
d. to
e. about
f. at
g. at
h. of
i. of
j. about

UNIT 2

Exercise 1

Sample answers

a. Yes. She's been to a lot of places, and done a lot of things in her life.
b. She has been writing for thirty-four years.
c. She's written short stories, poems and novels.
d. She's been to France, Germany, Italy, India, the Far East and America.
e. At the age of six, she wrote some short stories about animals.
   After the publication of her collection of poems she went to France and Germany.
   After her mother died, she went to Italy.
   While she was at university, she got married for the first time.
   While she was in her mid-twenties, her second novel was published.
   After her first marriage ended in divorce, she went to India and the Far East.
   Three years later she went to America.
   She got married for the second time at the age of thirty-four.
   Soon after moving to her present home in Hastings, she began writing her autobiography.
f. It lasted for seven years.
g. She has been married for six years.
h. She has been living there for three years.
i. She has been writing her autobiography for two years.

Exercise 2

a. How long have you been living there?
b. How long have you been playing tennis?
c. How long have you known him?
d. How long have you been working there?
e. How long have you had it?

Exercise 3

a. When did you move there?
b. How old were you when you started playing?
c. Where did you meet him?
d. Why did you decide to work in Italy?
e. How much did you pay for it?

Exercise 4

a. I'm writing
b. You've been sitting
c. I've decided
d. You've only been doing it
e. I've been offered
f. I've always wanted
g. I don't like
h. do you know
i. You've never been
j. are living

k. I've been trying
l. I've been
m. I've been turned down
n. you've been applying
o. I hope

Exercise 5

Sample answers

a. I've known her for two months.
b. I've been learning for three years.
c. Yes, I have. I've learned Spanish and Russian.
d. No, I haven't been to the cinema for weeks.
e. No, I haven't.
f. I've spent five pounds.
g. It's been very warm and sunny.
h. Yes, I have. I went to America a few weeks ago, actually.

Exercise 6

a. They offered him the job.
b. He sent the novel to ten well-known publishers.
c. Mrs Brown teaches us French three times a week.
d. Her grandfather left her five thousand pounds in his will.
e. The doctor is going to give the baby an injection.
f. I decided to write a letter of complaint to the editor of *The Times*.
g. She lent me a pen.
h. He took it to her.
i. She showed the letter to anyone that was interested.

Sample answers

j. The Director introduced the new teacher to the students.
k. She described the criminal to the police.
l. I explained the situation to the manager.
m. I reported the theft to the police.
n. She suggested an idea to her friends.

Exercise 7

storrup = glaimy (real word is hectic)
tragoon = zooly (real word is axe)
grumfit = pawdry (real word is dreary)
huckled = mag (real word is squeeze)
histit = bagshot (real word is rumour)
scrummy = blotchermer (real word is pebble)

Exercise 8

a. out of
b. away
c. back
d. up
e. over
f. out
g. out
h. in
i. out of
j. off

UNIT 3

Exercise 1

Sample answers

a. to find
b. opening
c. to tell
d. working
e. being
f. in finishing
g. having
h. him
i. manage to
j. in employing
k. to send
l. what to do
m. to leave
n. anyone
o. to say
p. to rain
q. to bring
r. to catch
s. to say
t. made him

Exercise 2

a. I was sorry to learn that your aunt had died.
b. He was anxious to know where we had been.
c. She was amazed to find that her husband was still alive.
d. I am disappointed to see that you're still smoking.
e. He was shocked to learn that he had nearly died.

Exercise 3

Sample answers

I want you to pick up the books/put away the clothes/make the bed/wash your face, etc.
She told them to pick up the books/put away the clothes, etc.
She asked them to make the bed/have a wash, etc.
She made them pick up the books/put away the clothes, etc.

Exercise 4

a. She admitted driving too fast through the town.
b. He offered to lend me some money.
c. He advised his daughter to accept the job.
d. He invited us to have a holiday in his country cottage.
e. She made me pay for the damage I had done.
f. She stopped smoking three years ago.
g. We stopped to buy some petrol.
h. I forgot to buy food for dinner, so we had to go out.
i. But I remembered to feed the cat.
j. I tried to learn the piano for years, but I was never very good.

Exercise 5

a. I don't want to.
b. I'd love to, but I'm afraid I can't.
c. But you promised to!
d. You're not allowed to.
e. You told me to.
f. He didn't ask me to.

ercise 6

mple answers

To learn English.
To make it taste better.
To lose weight.
To book a holiday.
To look for a new house.
To buy a bottle of wine.
To bet some money on a horse.
To get married.
To borrow a book.

ercise 7

ample answers

orse riding is good fun.
had a ride on Jane's horse.
rinking too much alcohol is bad for you.
Would you like to have a drink?
ooking for a new house can be very frustrating.
ave a look at this photograph. Do you recognize who
it is?
hate washing up.
'll just have a wash, then I'll be ready.
try to avoid quarrelling with anybody.
isten! They're having a quarrel!
Walking in the early morning is one of life's great
pleasures.
We had a lovely walk this morning.

Exercise 9

a. for	f. to
b. in	g. about
c. of	h. with
d. between	i. into
e. for	j. for

UNIT 4

Exercise 1

Sample answers

a. What sort of film is *Survival of the Fittest*?
b. Who's in it?
c. Who is it directed by?
d. What did Brian Henderson say about it?
e. Who said 'This is a film you mustn't miss'?
f. Where is it on?
g. How many times a day is it on?
h. When is there a late night show?
i. What is Anderson International advertising for?
j. What's the salary?
k. What sort of company is Anderson International?
l. How many people does it employ?
m. What sort of person are they looking for?
n. What should you do if you're interested in the job?

o. When was the house built?
p. What sort of house is it?
q. What sort of condition is it in?
r. How long is the garden?
s. How far is it to the shops and the tube?
t. How long does it take to get to Central London?

Exercise 2

a. What's she talking about?
b. What are you waiting for?
c. Who does he work for?
d. Who are you writing to?
e. Who was she angry with?
f. Who does the house belong to?
g. Who's the letter for?
h. Who did you stay with?

Exercise 3

Sample answers

a. I wonder how long it took him.
   I'd like to know why he did it.
b. I wonder why he's resigned.
   I can't imagine who's going to succeed him.
c. We don't know how old he is.
   I wonder how he does it.
d. Nobody knows how he did it.
   I wonder where he's gone to.
e. I wonder when they'll get it.
   I'd like to know why the government have decided to
   give them a rise.

Exercise 4

a – 4	b – 6	c – 8	d – 2	e – 7
f – 5	g – 1	h – 10	i – 9	j – 3

Exercise 5

a. of	g. with
b. for . . . for	h. from . . . to
c. with . . . for	i. about
d. for	j. to
e. of	k. at
f. of	l. for

Exercise 6: Ways of looking

a. watch . . . face   c. glance   e. gazed
b. stare   d. notice

Exercise 6: Ways of speaking

Sample answers

a. People scream if they are frightened, or very excited.
b. People cheer when they are happy, or when they want
   to encourage someone, for example, at a football match.
c. People swear when they hit their finger with a hammer.
d. People groan when they are in pain.
e. People cry when they are very upset.

Exercise 6: Ways of moving

Sample answers

	to limp	to stagger	to tiptoe	to march	to race	to crawl
Small steps	✓		✓			
Large steps				✓	✓	
Normal steps						
With difficulty	✓	✓	•			✓
Slowly	✓	✓	✓			✓
Fast				✓	✓	
Quietly			✓			
Loudly				✓	✓	
Without control	✓	✓				

Answers to Revision Test (1)

Question 1

a. to
b. be
c. refused
d. was sent
e. riding
f. why
g. did
h. would be able to
i. him
j. not
k. looking
l. was asked
m. being
n. have been writing
o. haven't received
p. getting
q. leaving
r. has been treated
s. Going
t. has done

Question 2

At last I have arrived here in New York! I'm very excited – everything is so big, and people move so fast. I'm sure I'll enjoy it very much. At the moment I'm staying in a hotel. It's quiet, so I sleep all right, not too expensive, and near the centre, which is very convenient. I'm thinking of looking for a small flat to rent. I would prefer to live in a flat rather than in a hotel. I don't think hotels are very nice places to stay for more than a few days, and in a flat you are more independent.

I haven't told you about my job. I'm working three days a week as a receptionist at another hotel near this one, called the Metropole. A lot of people who work in the hotel are Spanish or German, and their English isn't very good, either!

Yesterday I bought the book you asked me to get. When do you want me to send it? Let me know. Write to me soon. I'm looking forward to hearing from you.

Question 3

a. I like watching horror films very much.
b. But I am usually in bed when they are on.
c. I went to the bookshop to buy a collection of short stories that a friend of mine had recommended.
d. She gave her husband a silk tie for his birthday last year.
e. I don't understand why you didn't tell me immediately.
f. Most English families have a newspaper delivered to their house every morning.
g. I can never remember where I have put the letters that I have to reply to.
h. I'll check the report carefully this afternoon in my office.
i. They're getting married at three o'clock on Saturday afternoon in the small church where my wife and I were married.
j. I thought she spoke five languages fluently, but apparently she only speaks three.

Question 4

Sample answers

a. What did Walter Davidson see by the road?
b. What did he do when he saw her?
c. What was the weather like?
d. What had happen her?
e. Who did he con
f. Why did he contact him?
g. How many other people had seen the girl?
h. Why didn't Ian Nicholson report what he'd seen to the police?
i. Did the salesman stop when he saw the body?
j. Who told Mr Wright what had happened three hundred years earlier?

Question 5

a. disappeared   f. carefully
b. isolated   g. shocked
c. stopped suddenly   h. without success
d. cruel   i. nearly
e. he was shaking   j. extraordinary

Question 7

to disbelieve; useless; illegal; to unpack; unimportance;
unreliable; inefficiency; nonsense; to dislike; unnecessary;
impolite; to disappear; painless; inexperienced; to
disapprove; to unlock; untidy; immature; dishonest;
inaccurate; harmful; to disagree; disadvantage;
improbable; irresponsible.

Question 8

Odd man out

a. work   h. build   o. height   v. cows
b. though   i. down   p. want   w. said
c. home   j. worse   q. lose   x. doll
d. barn   k. prove   r. rough   y. wrong
e. phone   l. foot   s. shone   z. pear
f. owned   m. weak   t. sorry
g. lower   n. north   u. wood

UNIT 5

Exercise 1

a. were standing   h. thought
b. stood   i. were you doing
c. studied   j. did you do
d. was studying   k. did you do
e. was raining   l. were you doing
f. rained   m. was dying
g. was thinking   n. died

Exercise 2

Sample answers

a. because she had lost his keys.
b. He had spent it all on cars and women.
c. because she had stolen from her employer.
d. He had just had some awful news.
e. because he had got lost on the way to the church.
f. I had seen her somewhere before.
g. although I had spent weeks revising.
h. who had just been awarded a scholarship to
university.
i. because I had never flown before.
j. His car had been completely wrecked.

Exercise 3

a. had read   d. had never played
b. had been reading   e. had cooked
c. had been playing   f. had been working

Exercise 4

a. didn't recognize . . . hadn't seen
b. had finished . . . went
c. arrived . . . had gone
d. had eaten . . . got
e. had been awarded . . . was
f. died . . . had reigned
g. was touched . . . had looked
h. wrote . . . had not arrived
i. came . . . had broken
j. refused . . . had been

Exercise 5

c. Essential   g. Essential
d. Essential   h. Essential
e. Optional   i. Essential
f. Essential   j. Optional

Exercise 6

a. was driving   h. had swerved
b. overtook   i. Have you spoken
c. was travelling   j. arrived
d. was going   k. was trying
e. have never seen   l. has/had been drinking
f. saw   m. has broken
g. had crashed

Exercise 7

11   4   1   2   8   9   7   6   5   3   10   12   13

Sample answers

Mr Barron was reunited with his children after he had
had a phone call from Bernadette.

Mr Barron discovered where they were staying after a
friend of his wife had phoned.

As soon as Bernadette had written the note, the children
left home.

When they had all had breakfast, Mr Barron said he
hoped his wife would come back soon.

Exercise 10

a. for . . . from . . . to   f. Until
b. at   g. by
c. During . . . at   h. in
d. in . . . on   i. at
e. since   j. At

UNIT 6

Exercise 1

a. Some . . . any
b. some . . . any
c. some
d. some . . . any
e. any
f. any
g. some
h. any
i. some
j. any

Exercise 2

a. anywhere
b. anyone
c. someone
d. anything
e. somewhere
f. anything
g. somewhere
h. somewhere
i. nobody
j. Everything

Exercise 3

a. There isn't much employment for school leavers.
b. He couldn't give me many details.
c. When I moved into my flat, I had very little furniture.
d. There isn't much accommodation to rent in this town.
e. I haven't got much luggage. It's in the boot.
f. I had a few minutes to spare, so I browsed round a bookshop.
g. Very few experiments have been done to find out the cause.
h. It's very quiet in my area. There isn't much traffic.

Exercise 4

a. There are a few left in the tin.
b. I have little time for relaxation.
c. Few people give more to charity.
d. There's a little butter
e. he has little chance of success
f. you need a few fillings
g. but few of them ever worked properly
h. She just had a little soup

Exercise 5

Sample answers

a. Women have less free time than men.
b. Men do very little housework.
c. Hardly any men do any washing or ironing.
d. Only one man in twenty prepares the evening meal.
e. Seventeen per cent of men wash the dishes in the evening.
f. Most repairs in the household are done by men.
g. Britons have more money now than ten years ago.
h. Britons smoke fewer cigarettes, and are eating healthier foods.
i. Spain is the most popular place to go on holiday.
j. There were four times as many divorces among husbands in unskilled manual jobs as among professional classes.
k. Fewer than two in five divorced women were receiving maintenance from their former husbands.
l. There were fewer marriages in 1983 than in 1982.

Exercise 6

a. are
b. Britain
c. working
d. time
e. than
f. on
g. The
h. likely
i. a
j. Sunday
k. newspapers
l. In
m. adults
n. holiday
o. risen

Exercise 8

a. injured
b. wound
c. pain . . . hurts
d. injured
e. aches
f. wounded
g. painful
h. hurts

Exercise 10

a. by . . . on
b. in
c. in
d. On
e. on . . . under
f. in
g. in
h. for
i. in . . . in
j. in

UNIT 7

Exercise 1

a. I'll look it up in the directory
b. We're going to rest.
c. It will/is going to be cold at first, then it will/is going to get a little warmer this afternoon, and this evening there'll be some light showers.
d. We're going to modernize it . . . we're going to turn it
e. what will/is your party do/going to do about unemployment . . . as we most certainly will be, we are going to create
f. I'll give her a ring . . . I'll/I'm going to be late
g. We'll cross
h. What are you going to call it

Exercise 2

Corrected mistakes

a. I'll get a cloth
b. What will you do/are you going to do/are you doing
c. I'm going back to university
d. Will I disturb/be disturbing you
e. I'll miss my appointment
f. I'll do/I'm going to do a retraining scheme

Exercise 3

a. I'm coming
b. I'm going to see/ I'm seeing
c. Will you be/ are you
d. I won't be
e. I'm going
f. are you going
g. is opening
h. are you going
i. I'm not back/I won't be back
j. does your plane get in
k. I'll be/I could be
l. I'll see
m. We'll have finished
n. I'll see you

Exercise 4

a. He'll be working . . . he won't hear
b. it may/might/could rain
c. we won't disturb/be disturbing . . . She won't be working
d. it might/could work
e. She won't come
f. They may/might not like
g. the plane will be delayed
h. and might bite
i. what will happen . . . I'll go . . . she'll be having a bath or doing her hair . . . I'll have to wait
j. Suzy will be wearing

Exercise 5

a. I won't be . . . there is
b. won't go . . . they have had
c. You'll phone . . . you go
d. When are you going
   When I've finished . . . It'll take
e. you don't hurry . . . we'll be
f. I'll come . . . you find/have found
g. you'll feel . . . you've taken
h. We'll have . . . the guests arrive/have arrived
i. You won't forget . . . you go
j. I won't let . . . I've been told

Exercise 6

a. about   f. on
b. in   g. in
c. from   h. to
d. to . . . about i. about
e. to/with   j. to . . . about

Exercise 7

1 i	6 g	11 b
2 l	7 c	12 h
3 f	8 a	13 m
4 j	9 d	
5 k	10 e	

UNIT 8

Exercise 1

a. (nothing)	i. that	
b. that	j. which	
c. who	k. that . . . which	
d. which	l. whose	
e. where	m. who	
f. (nothing)	n. which	
g. who	o. (nothing)	
h. (nothing)		

Exercise 2

Sample answers

a. I've ever met.
b. that doesn't need any work doing to it.
c. I cook
d. that I usually go to
e. who make too much noise.
f. who don't thank you

Exercise 3

a. My wife, who works as a journalist, is an excellent cook.
b. My daughter, who works in New York, is getting married soon. (I have one daughter.)
   My daughter who works in New York is getting married soon. (I have more than one daughter.)
c. The engagement, which was announced last week, came as a bit of a shock.
d. The man she's getting married to is an artist.
e. It doesn't seem to me that artists are the kind of people who can be relied on to provide an income.
f. Artists who are unproductive are not much use to anyone. (Only those artists who are unproductive; not all artists.)
   Artists, who are unproductive, are not much use to anyone. (All artists are unproductive.)
g. My daughter has been married once before, which means she should know what she's doing.
h. Her previous marriage, which ended in divorce, was to a Spaniard.
i. Her mother and father-in-law, who were always exceptionally kind, were very upset when the marriage broke down.
j. The children who spoke Spanish went to live with their father after the divorce. (Not all the children — only those that spoke Spanish.)
   The children, who spoke Spanish, went to live with their father after the divorce. (All the children spoke Spanish.)

Exercise 4

Sample answer

The job that I have recently started is as a sales representative with a company that produces garden furniture. The company, called 'Sunnosit', is based in Thornton, a small town in the Midlands. The area manager, who has been with the company for over thirty years, is due to retire next year, which means I might get his job if I do well. One great advantage is having a company car, which I have to have, because the job involves visiting different parts of the country. My colleagues, who I get on well with, are quite ambitious, which means the atmosphere at work is rather competitive. I don't mind. Apart from that, the job is fine.

Exercise 5

a. disgusting
b. interested
c. annoying
d. horrified
e. embarrassing
f. satisfied
g. confused
h. shocking
i. disappointing
j. amazing

Exercise 6

a. The train standing at platform 6
b. People living in high-rise blocks
c. The money given to old-age pensioners
d. The man sent to repair my central heating
e. My aunt, knowing how much I liked chocolates, bought me

Exercise 7

a. hiding
b. standing . . . looking
c. crying
d. hidden
e. saying
f. wanting
g. Growing
h. stealing
i. stolen
j. injuring . . . tearing

Exercise 8

a. terribly/awfully
b. absolutely
c. rather/quite
d. rather/terribly
e. absolutely
f. terribly/awfully . . . rather/quite . . . quite/totally
g. absolutely . . . rather/terribly
h. terribly/awfully
i. rather/terribly/awfully
j. terribly/awfully

Exercise 9

This elegant garden trolley is a must for every household. Designed by our master craftsmen in Italy and manufactured in Germany, this trolley will grace your garden, and be the envy of your neighbours! It's everything you need in a trolley – light and easy to steer, yet strong and weather-proof, with its frame made of reinforced, long-lasting plastic and its top deck finished in non-scratch vinyl. It has two levels for the food, glasses, crockery, cutlery and the rest. The integral bottle recess could even be filled with ice to keep the drinks chilled. For the winter months, it can be folded away, but you'll be tempted to use it indoors! Measures 30" × 24½" × 30".

Exercise 11

a. a three-hour walk
b. a fifty-thousand pound house
c. a twenty-five minute programme
d. a five-hour wait
e. a five-star hotel
f. a sixty-minute cassette
g. a sixty-watt bulb

Exercise 12

a. against
b. out of
c. beside
d. beneath
e. below
f. behind
g. on to
h. towards
i. over
j. among
k. over . . . across
l. above

Answers to Revision Test (2)

Question 1

Sample answers

a. who
b. settled
c. had been trying
d. several
e. which
f. until
g. had been
h. which
i. few
j. has been developed
k who
l. some
m. covered
n. will find
o. may/might/could
p. offering
q. will have been completed
r. little

Question 2

I asked the receptionist for help, but he couldn't give me any information.

I had a very nice day yesterday. I didn't have to go to work because it was my day off, so I went to see some friends instead.

Jeremy Peterson, the Hollywood actor, died at home yesterday. He had been ill since 1985, and had had several operations.

A What are you doing tonight?
B Nothing. Why?
A Would you like to go out for a meal?
B What a lovely idea! Where shall we go?
A It's a surprise. I'll pick you up at 7.00. Is that all right?
B Fine! How exciting!
A If you aren't ready, I'll go without you.
B Don't worry. I'll be ready.

e. The film was absolutely wonderful. I was so excited. I had no idea how it was going to end.

f. Put your money somewhere safe. You might lose it if you aren't careful.

g. I've had so little spare time recently – I think I've forgotten how to relax.

h. I'm sure that's the man whose car I bumped into last week. He didn't stop to give me his address, which I found very strange. After all, the accident was my fault.

i. The weather forecast said it's going to rain tomorrow. If it does, we won't be able to go out. Never mind. The forecast might be wrong. It often is.

Question 3

a. **B**	e. **A**	i. **C**	
b. **A**	f. **C**	j. **C**	
c. **C**	g. **B**		
d. **B**	h. **A**		

Question 4

Skyway Tours Ltd.,
117 Brompton Court Road,
Cambridge
CB2 4JK

19 October 1986

Mr James Bradley,
The Towers,
Homefield Road,
Little Chalfont,
Buckinghamshire
GR4 8QJ

Dear Mr Bradley,

Thank you for your letter of 3 October, which was forwarded to me by Sheila Brown of our Complaints Department, to whom you wrote regarding your recent holiday on the Caribbean island of St Lucia.

I was sorry to learn that the holiday was not to your satisfaction, and having made certain enquiries, I must admit that your reasons for complaint seem well-founded. I personally got in touch with Mr Peter Thompson, the manager of The Plaza Hotel, where you stayed with your wife and children, and he informed me that your room had not been prepared to our normal high standard. I understand the laundry service was inadequate because the washing machine broke down. Its motor has now been replaced. This would explain why your wife's clothes were damaged.

Regarding the play area which you saw advertised in our brochure, it had apparently not been possible to complete this on time, which explains why there was a lot of builders' material in the area near the swimming pool. I was sorry to learn of your children's accident, and I hope they have recovered from their injuries.

In view of all these misfortunes, I hope you will accept my sincere apologies and a refund of half the total cost of your holiday.

Yours sincerely,
Malcolm Green
Director

Question 5

a. reliable	n. whole
b. plain	o. resources
c. fine	p. pressure
d. swallow	q. rises . . . sets
e. plaster	r. stare
f. stitches	s. ancestors
g. stroke	t. nightmare
h. shiver	u. vineyard
i. sunburnt	v. leisure
j. wise	w. bad-tempered
k. grateful	x. well-behaved
l. batteries	y. addicted
m. sale	z. cereals

Question 6

continent	1	interesting	1
Indian	1	vehicle	1
bilingual	4	stability	2
Chinese	3	wondered	5
experience	2	departure	4
competitive	2	several	5
creative	4	chemical	1
developed	4	convenient	2
accurate	1	disease	3
vegetable	1	ancestors	1
biography	2	recipe	1
January	1	statistics	4
colleague	5	medicine	5
successful	4	literature	1
managed	5	depressed	3
emergency	2		

UNIT 9

Exercise 1

a. He can't have retired yet.
b. He can't be very well off.
c. He might have spent all his money when he was younger.
d. He must do a lot of gardening.
e. He must have read a lot of books about gardening.
f. He must be working in his garden.
g. He might be talking to Miss Appleby.
h. No, it can't be Miss Appleby.
i. They might be having an argument.
j. Harry might owe the other man some money.
k. They must have gone inside.
l. Harry must have killed him!
m. It can't have been Harry who was shot.
n. This must be the police arriving.
o. They must have been making a film!

Exercise 2

You can't have seen Alice in town yesterday. She went abroad last week.

You can't have been served in a restaurant by Tessa. She's a school-teacher.

Sheila must be thinking of moving. There's a *For Sale* notice up outside her house.

Anita must have got engaged to Alan. I saw her looking at wedding rings yesterday.

Pat can't have hurt her leg. I've just seen her playing tennis.

Jenny can't be going out with Tom. She told me she didn't like him.

Mary must be having her flat decorated. There's a strong smell of paint coming from next door.

Exercise 3

Sample answers

a. The father must hope that his son will be more responsible.
b. They might want to see if their relationship will last.
c. He must be mentally disturbed.
d. The surgeon must be his mother.

Exercise 4

a. might/could have
b. might/could have
c. must have
d. must have
e. might/could be
f. might/could be
g. must be
h. can't have
i. must have
j. might not have
k. may/might/could be

Exercise 5

Sample answers

1 The husband of a teenage girl must have written the letter. His daughter must be staying out late at night. He must have told his daughter to get home earlier. He might have said that if she doesn't, she'll have to leave home.

2 It must have been written by a woman who is about to get married to a man who has unpleasant eating habits and bad breath.

3 It must have been written by a woman whose husband keeps putting off doing jobs around the house.

4 It must have been written by a lonely girl, probably a teenager. Her friends might have been unkind to her.

Exercise 6

a – 5   b – 2   c – 8   d – 3   e – 4
f – 9   g – 1   h – 7   i – 6   j – 10

a. we talked it over
b. We tried it out
c. I've really gone off it
d. call if off
e. Why don't you give it up?
f. I'll look into it
g. You'll soon get over it
h. to turn it down
i. you look after it
j. I can't work it out

Exercise 7

Sample answers

sir – a waiter or taxi driver
mate – a friend or a shop keeper
old boy – a friend or colleague
guv'nor – a taxi driver, especially in London
Doctor – his patients
Richard – his wife, colleagues or friends
Dick – this is a nickname, so a close friend
Daddy – his children
Pop – his children (especially American)
Grandpa – his grandchildren
Mr Henderson – anyone in a formal situation
Henderson – a colleague (this is quite old-fashioned now)

ma'am – a waiter or (high-class) shop keeper
luv – a bus conductor or market-stall holder
dear – her husband or a close friend
darling – her husband
Elizabeth – friends or colleagues
Liz – this is a nickname, so a close friend
Mummy – her children
Mum – her children, perhaps older children
Mom – her children (especially American)
Gran – her grandchildren
Miss – the children in her class at work
Mrs Henderson – anyone in a formal situation

UNIT 10

Exercise 1

a. big-headed
b. moody
c. cheerful
d. dishonest
e. lazy
f. loyal
g. obstinate
h. rude
i. unsociable
j. naive

Exercise 2

Sample answers

a. She always looks on the bright side of everything.
b. He's always slurping his soup.
c. He'll risk everything and go off travelling for six months at a time.
d. They're always inviting us in for a meal.
e. When she brushes her teeth, she'll leave the tap running until the sink overflows.
f. He smiles and laughs from morning till night.
g. She's got a word to say to everyone.
h. You're always complaining about everything I do.
i. He just can't look people in the eye.

Exercise 3

Sample answers

a. If he had some sweets, he wouldn't give any away.
b. She used to leave her room in a terrible mess.
c. Sometimes she'd go off on a hike for the whole day.
d. His parents used to give him everything he asked for.
e. One of them always used to be in some play or other.
f. She'd give them especially good marks.
g. If you dropped anything on the carpet, she'd make you clean it up.
h. I used to play for my school at all sorts of sports.

Exercise 4

Sample answers

a. My grandfather would sit in his rocking chair
b. My grandmother would get very cross
c. She'll get the lead and she'll tug at my trousers
d. But she *will* run in other people's gardens and pull up their flowers.
e. we would be cut off for weeks on end, and we'd have to live
f. she'll take the batteries out
g. But then she *will* forget where she put the batteries.
h. He'd buy me flowers every Friday, and he'd write poems

Exercise 5

a. 3
b. 3
c. 2
d. 1
e. 1
f. 1
g. 2
h. 3
i. 1
j. 1
k. 1
l. 3
m. 1
n. 1
o. 3

Exercise 6

a. take
b. that
c. breakfast
d. enough
e. empty
f. made
g. before
h. much
i. depended
j. supper
k. rubbing
l. became/grew/got
m. so
n. return

Exercise 7

a. get used
b. got divorced
c. getting married
d. get lost
e. are lost
f. is getting ready
   have been ready
g. am getting better slowly
h. was not used
   am used
i. got to know
j. aren't used
k. Getting divorced
l. is better/is getting better

Exercise 8

a. to waste time/food/money/energy/an opportunity/paper
   to spend time/money
b. strange person/behaviour/country
   odd number/socks/man out/jobs
c. common cold/sense/knowledge
   plain face/clothes/paper/food
d. big nose/mistake/decision/man/building
   great man/writer/friend
e. fast car/worker/lane of a motorway/food restaurant
   quick meal/temper

Exercise 10

a. out of
b. on with
c. down on
d. away from
e. back on
f. down on
g. up to
h. out of
i. up against
j. up to
k. in with
l. away with

UNIT 11

Exercise 1

Sample answers

a. He shouldn't have been driving home.
   He should have taken a taxi.
b. He shouldn't have tried to stop the man.
   He should have let him go.
c. She should have fastened her bag.
   She shouldn't have left it unattended.

d. You shouldn't have left it in your car.
   You should have shut the window.
e. She should have bought a ticket.
   She shouldn't have got on the train without one.
f. They shouldn't have let their son play with matches.
   They should have insured their house.

Exercise 2

Sample answers

If he had been looking where he was going, he would
   have seen the dog.

If he had seen the dog, he wouldn't have tripped over it.

If he hadn't bumped into the child, the ice cream
   wouldn't have dropped.

If the ice cream hadn't dropped on to the ground, he
   wouldn't have slipped on it.

If the man hadn't fallen off the ladder, the paint wouldn't
   have fallen on to the policeman.

Exercise 3

a. go . . . will write
b. are watered . . . die
c. were . . . would go
d. are . . . will be stopped
e. had been sitting . . . would have been killed
f. don't like . . . is undercooked
g. don't hurry . . . will get
h. had . . . would disappear
i. was . . . would look
j. we had gone . . . it would have been . . . we would
   have
k. she had been wearing . . . she wouldn't have been
   hurt
l. see . . . I'll give
m. could . . . I would open
n. I hadn't been ill . . . she hadn't been the doctor . . .
   we wouldn't have met . . . we wouldn't have got
   married . . . our children wouldn't have been born
o. you are able/have been able . . . are

Exercise 4

Sample answers

a. I wish the weather was nicer.
b. I wish we could go swimming.
c. I wish we hadn't gone to the Ritz.
d. I wish there was something to do in the evening.
e. I wish we had a television.
f. I wish we had gone to Spain.
g. I wish they hadn't persuaded me to come to Westby.
h. I wish the children didn't/wouldn't keep asking me for
   money.
i. I wish my wife would help with the children.
j. I wish we didn't have to get up at 7.00.

Exercise 5

Sample answers

If he knew how to behave at interviews, he might get a
   job.

If he didn't smoke so much, he would be able to go to
   football matches.

He wishes he could go abroad.

Exercise 7

a. in	f. from	k. to
b. to	g. for	l. with
c. at	h. for	m. of
d. of	i. to	n. on
e. on	j. about/of	o. from

UNIT 12

Exercise 1

a. A	n. The
b. the	o. the
c. a	p. the
d. a	q. (nothing)
e. (nothing)	r. a
f. The	s. A
g. the	t. a
h. (nothing)	u. the
i. the	v. the
j. (nothing)	w. a
k. the	x. a
l. the	y. (nothing)
m. the	

Exercise 2

a. lamb
b. a lamb
c. a cake
d. cake
e. very fine cloth
f. a cloth . . . tea
g. a talk . . . the Russian revolution
h. talk
i. Service
j. The Health Service
k. *The Times*
l. Time and tide
m. poetry
n. a poem
o. ice
p. The ice

Exercise 3

a. a
b. the
c. a . . . The . . . (nothing) . . . the
d. a

, the . . . a

, a . . . the . . . (nothing) . . . a . . . the

, the

, A . . . a . . . (nothing)

The . . . a . . . the . . . (nothing) . . . (nothing) . . .
the

, the . . . (nothing)

Exercise 4

a. you've got lovely fingers

b. interested in history

c. What lovely weather

d. Some people came to see
   but the people who saw it on Sunday morning

e. to buy some bread
   at the shops

f. in bad weather

g. The people who live

h. about unemployment

Exercise 5

a. ten pence a pound

b. fifteen thousand pounds a year

c. thirty miles an hour

d. three pills a day

e. eighty pounds a night

f. forty cigarettes a day

g. one pound ninety a gallon

h. two pounds fifty a metre

i. five flights a day

Exercise 6

a. (nothing)   h. (nothing) . . . (nothing)

b. the   i. a

c. (nothing)   j. (nothing)

d. a   k. (nothing)

e. the   l. an

f. (nothing)   m. the

g. (nothing)   n. the

Exercise 7

a. The same   i. go-ahead

b. Not the same   j. outlook

c. Not the same   k. drawback

d. Not the same   l. upbringing

e. Not the same   m. outcry

f. The same   n. breakthrough

g. Not the same   o. break-up

h. Not the same

Exercise 9

a. out of   f. In

b. in   g. out of

c. for   h. at

d. On   i. on . . . by

e. In   j. on

Answers to Revision Test (3)

Question 1

Sample answers

a. who   k. of

b. get   l. were ordered

c. a   m. on

d. must   n. could

e. missing   o. would

f. had hit   p. would

g. would/might/could have killed   q. used

h. the   r. must

i. used   s. had told

j. should   t. used

Question 2

a. C   h. A   o. A   v. C

b. B   i. D   p. B   w. B

c. D   j. B   q. D   x. D

d. A   k. C   r. A   y. C

e. D   l. C   s. C   z. B

f. A   m. D   t. B

g. B   n. C   u. D

Question 3

Sample answers

a. I suggest that you should cut down on your spending.

b. I wish you had told me that I'd upset you.

c. Your car might have been stolen.

d. You should be working.

e. He's getting used to working at night.

f. He apologized for being late.

g. This is the first time I've seen this film.

h. I can't run as fast as Peter.

i. She asked me if I had done that sort of work before.

j. She can't have done it on purpose.

Question 4

a. endless   f. competitors

b. misunderstanding   g. unexplored

c. uneconomical   h. poverty

d. astonishing   i. speciality

e. comparison   j. carelessness

Question 5

Sample answers

a. Thank you for your letter, which arrived yesterday.

b. As I'm sure you can imagine, we have been very busy
   recently, having just moved into our new house.

c. We are slowly settling in, although it will be a long
   time before everything is finished.

d. Jack is putting down the living room carpet at the
   moment, and tonight we are having a house-warming
   party.

e. I was sorry to hear you couldn't come. If we had told you earlier, you could have put off your mother's visit.

f. You said in your letter that you'd like to visit us in the summer.

g. I'm sure we will have finished all the things we want to do in the house by then.

h. We have seen exactly the kind of carpet we want to put upstairs, and we are going to buy it tomorrow.

Question 6

a. away . . . at
b. up . . . out . . . at
c. on . . . on . . . out
d. of . . . from
e. of . . . on
f. to . . . in
g. from . . . in
h. of . . . at . . . in
i. on . . . by
j. out
k. for . . . on . . . up
l. across . . . at . . . out
m. against . . . down
n. in . . . with . . . about
o. up . . . to
p. up . . . for . . . off . . . for . . . of
q. with . . . back . . . back
r. across . . . with . . . on
s. for . . . to
t. in . . . with . . . on

Question 7

Corrections

a. countries
b. anniversary
c. consistent
d. travelled
e. accommodation
f. planned
g. current
h. passed
i. bathing
j. quarrelling
k. helpful
l. allowed
m. practice
n. suffering

Question 8

Stressed words

a. did
b. I
c. John
d. ages
e. told
f. You
g. in
h. New York
i. I
j. didn't
k. soon
l. going
m. been
n. sons
o. three . . . one

94